Morphology of the *Cantar de Mio Cid*

JACK J. HIMELBLAU

SCRIPTA HUMANISTICA ®

Publisher and Distributor

SCRIPTA HUMANISTICA®

1383 Kersey Lane,
Potomac, Maryland 20854, USA
Phone: 301-294-7949
Fax: 301-424-9584
Internet: www.scriptahumanistica.com
Email: info@scriptahumanistica.com

® 2010 JACK J. HIMELBLAU

S.H: # 164
I.S.B.N. 1-882528-55-7
Price: $69.95

**Printed in the United States of America
2010**

Morphology of the *Cantar de Mio Cid*

SCRIPTA HUMANISTICA ®

Directed by
BRUNO M. DAMIANI
The Catholic University of America

ADVISORY BOARD

Carlos Alvar
Université de Genève

Samuel G. Armistead
*University of California
(Davis)*

Juan Bautista Avalle-Arce
*University of California
(Santa Barbara)*

Theodore Beardsley
*The Hispanic Society of
America*

Frederick A. De Armas
*Andrew W. Mellon Professor
in Humanities
University of Chicago*

Dante Della Terza
Harvard University

Frédéric Deloffre
Université de Paris-Sorbonne

Charles B. Faulhaber
*University of California
(Berkeley)*

Edward H. Friedman
Vanderbilt University

Michael P. Iarocci
*University of California
(Berkeley)*

Louis Imperiale
*University of Missouri
(Kansas City)*

John Keller
University of Kentucky

Richard Kinkade
University of Arizona

Adelaida López de Martínez
*University of Nebraska
(Lincoln)*

Cardinal Francesco Marchisano
*Pontificia Commissione
per la Conservazione del
Patrimonio Artistico e
Storico della Chiesa.
Città del Vaticano*

Martín de Riquer
Real Academia Española

Giuliano Soria
*Università di Roma
 Presidente
Premio Grinzane Cavour*

Paolo Valesio
Yale University

TO

Enrique Anderson Imbert and *Ismael Puerta Flores*

IN MEMORIAM

ACKNOWLEDGMENTS

I am grateful to David Brown, editor of publications at Aris and Phillips, for permission to reprint English translations from The *Poem of Mio Cid*, translated, introduction, and commentary by Peter Such and John Hodgkinson (Warminster: Aris and Phillips, 1987).

A variant of the analysis of the tale dealing with the exile of Rodrigo Díaz de Vivar, the Cid, has appeared in "The *Cantar de Mio Cid*: A Morphological-Syntagmatic Analysis of the Exile of the Cid," *eHumanista: Journal of Medieval and Early Modern Iberian Studies* 6 (2006): 1–18 <http//www.ehumanista.ucsb.edu/>.

A generous grant from the College of Liberal and Fine Arts of The University of Texas at San Antonio has assisted in meeting the publication costs of this volume.

Contents

Chapter 1.   Preliminary Remarks................. 1

Chapter 2.   The Number of Tales in the *Cantar de Mio Cid*.....................….....7

Chapter 3.   The Tale of the Exile of Rodrigo Díaz, the Cid............................... 9

Chapter 4.   The Tale of Fernando González and Diego González, the Infantes of Carrión..............................…...65

Chapter 5.   The Tale of the Revenge of the Cid on the Infantes of Carrión and the Remarriage of Doña Elvira and Doña Sol to the Infante of Navarre and Infante of Aragón 108

Conclusion...124

Appendix 127

Notes..160

Works Consulted....................................170

Chapter 1. Preliminary Remarks

Vladimir Propp's ground-breaking *Morphology of the Folktale* applies to Russian fairy tales whose content contains elements of magic. His study reveals that the syntagmatic progression of narrative functions in these tales is both orderly and uniform.[1] In the new introduction to the second English edition of the M*orphology*, Alan Dundes posits that Propp's structural approach may very well be suited to narratives that fall outside the province of folktale and fairy-tale genres. Specifically, Dundes raises the following intriguing question: "[W]hat is the relationship of Propp's *Morphology* to the structure of epic?" (*Morphology* xiv). In the present study, I shall attempt to answer Dundes's above query with respect to medieval Spanish epic poetry by conducting a detailed, intrinsic analysis of the fourteenth-century Per Abbat copy of the manuscript of the anonymously written *Cantar de Mio Cid*.[2]

In my syntagmatic analysis of the tales that comprise the *Cantar de Mio Cid*, I adopt Propp's critical terminology as well as his symbols to describe and designate the functions of the characters in this epic poem.[3] Propp's methodological approach provides a thorough analysis of the basis and structure of the aforementioned traditional diegetic principle of diachronic deployment of fictive events in narratology. His systematic exposition renders a formal modus operandi that methodically and accurately describes the diegetic strands that comprise the unity of a narrative poem such as the *Cantar de Mio Cid*. The symbols Propp employs provide precise, schematic means to encode logically the sequence of narrative actions. His critical lexica, in turn, present clear and concise descriptors, both unemotional and uniform (universal), that elucidate vague structural aspects of diegetic events such as exposition, development, and suspense, in functional terms that reflect the actions of the characters, such as absentation, trickery, villainy, struggle, and difficult task.

Several Proppian notions form the basis of this study. In his *Morphology*, Propp maintains that the Russian fairy tales subject of his analysis—that is, the Aarne-Thompson Tale Types (TT) 300 through 749, classified under the rubric of "Tales of Magic," dealing with supernatural personages, objects, and events (Dundes, *Morphology* xiv)—evidence a total of thirty-one functions for a complete fairy tale (64). Following an initial situation that does not constititute a function, designated by the Greek letter alpha (α) (25–26), the latter thirty-one functions, Propp avers, succeed each other in a strict sequential order (22). Moreover, Propp asserts that "[t]he absence of certain functions does not change the order of the rest" (22). The abridged definitions of thirty of the above thirty-one functions——function XIX lacks a definition—and their respective symbols (26–64) are as follows:

    I: absentation (β)
    II: interdiction (γ)
    III: violation (δ)
    IV: reconnaissance (ε)
    V: delivery (ζ)
    VI: trickery (η)
    VII: complicity (θ)
    VIII: villainy (A)
    VIIIa: lack (a)
    IX: mediation, the connective incident (B)
    X: the beginning of a counteraction (C)
    XI: departure (↑)
    XII: the first function of the donor (D)
    XIII: the hero's reaction (E)
    XIV: provision or receipt of a magical agent (F)
    XV: spatial transference between two kingdoms, guidance (G)
    XVI: struggle (H)
    XVII: branding (J)
    XVIII: victory (I)
    XIX: [the liquidation of the initial misfortune or lack] (K)
    XX: return (↑)
    XXI: pursuit, chase (Pr)
    XXII: rescue (Rs)
    XXIII: unrecognized arrival (o)
    XXIV: unfounded claims (L)
    XXV: difficult task (M)
    XXVI: solution (N)
    XXVII: recognition (Q)
    XXVIII: exposure (Ex)

XXIX: transfiguration (T)
XXX: punishment (U)
XXXI: wedding (W)

Propp underscores that "[f]unctions of characters serve as stable, constant elements in a tale, independent of how and by whom they are fulfilled" (21). Furthermore, Propp states that "[f]unction is understood as an act of character, defined from the point of view of its significance for the course of the action" (21).

Directly related to the above view of "function" is that of "move," still another Proppian notion that I incorporate in this study. This concept logically provides the means by which one can map out the distinct diegetic parts whose sum constitutes a complete tale. According to Propp:

> Morphologically, a tale (skázka) may be termed any development proceeding from villainy (A) or a lack (a), through intermediary functions to marriage (W*), or to other functions employed as a denouement. Terminal functions are at times a reward (F), a gain or in general the liquidation of misfortune (K), an escape from pursuit (Rs)... This type of development is termed by us a *move* (*xod*). Each new act of villainy, each new lack creates a new move. One tale may have several moves, [*sic*] and when analyzing a text, one must first of all determine the number of moves of which it consists. (92)

The clear implication of Propp's above definition of "move" is that a tale starts in a state of equilibrium or rest, that this state suffers a disturbance and passes into a state of disequilibrium, and that the latter diegetically demands, in turn, a terminal resolution of the disturbance, leaving the tale once more in a state of equilibrium. Propp's functional (structural) analysis rests on the principle of cause and effect, an approach rooted in the Poetics of Aristotle. In the long and short of it, Propp is an Aristotelian.

Technical Diegetic Features in the Cantar de Mio Cid
The diegetic events in the epic poem mainly unfold diachronically, but some actions are synchronic, as well. Among the latter, for example, are scenes of the various military actions in which the men led by the Cid and those led by his officers engage the Moors in military battles. I relegate such synchronic, military moments to a minor status and shall mention them only in passing. Other instances of synchronism are rather flagrant, overtly employing, for example, the "meanwhile, back at the ranch" narrative device: I shall duly report such instances wherever they occur within my analysis of the *Cantar de Mio Cid*.

Several other items of technical narrative interest are relevant to this study. Consistency in the deployment of point of view is not a critical structural consideration in the *Cantar de Mio Cid*. In the epic poem the narrator switches from an omniscient angle of vision of zero focalization to that of a first-person singular or first-person plural point of observation without any concern for uniformity. Regardless of the perspective the narrator adopts at any given moment, the point of view remains consistently omniscient. Passages of spatial and temporal foreshortening are, as Edmund de Chasca has pointed out (89–94), plentiful and the means by which the narrator achieves these effects are multiple. The narrator may place some of the Cid's men in Carrión in one line and in Valencia in the next, or he may state that a character travels "de día e de noch" (l. 2690) ["by day and by night"].[4] In other instances, the narrator, in one line, may simply inform the reader that the Cid has rested near a city, such as Alcocer, for fifteen weeks or that he laid siege to a city, such as Valencia, for nine months; in the next line he may state that the city capitulated in the tenth month. The narrator, also, may end a section of his tale by stating that two married couple (for example, don Fernando and don Diego, the infantes of Carrión, and their respective wives, doña Elvira and doña Sol) lived contentedly for almost two years.

There are, also, incidents of dramatic irony in the *Cantar de Mio Cid*. A case in point is when the Cid pawns two chests to Jewish businessmen Raquel and Vidas, in Move 2 of Tale 1, The Tale of the Exile of Rodrigo Díaz, the Cid. In this tale, the reader knows more than the two Jewish characters about the contents of the chests. Another instance occurs in Move 1 of Tale 11, The Tale of Don Fernando and Don Diego, the

Infantes of Carrión, where the reader learns of the materialistic reason that move the infantes of Carrión to want to marry the Cid's daughters, whereas King Alfonso and the Cid are ignorant of the infantes' motive. A third case takes place in Move 8 of Tale 11, in which the two brothers of Carrión emphasize to the nobles attending King Alfonso's court in Toledo that the inferior social status of doña Elvira and doña Sol make them unworthy of being their wives. However, the reader and King Alfonso know that the infantes never broached this issue when they, with the assistance of the king, had sought to contract marriage with the daughters of the Cid.

Finally, apostrophes to the reader appear sprinkled abundantly throughout the epic poem. In some instances the apostrophes to the reader constitute formulaic means by which the narrator abruptly shifts from one subject matter to another. De Chasca cites four such cases: "*D'iffantes de Carrión yo vos quiero contra*; *Quiérovos dezir del que en buena çinxo espada*; *Dezir vos quiero nuevas de allent partes del mar, / de aquel rey Yúcef que en Marruecos está*; *Alabandos ivan ifantes de Carrión / mas yo vos diré d'aquel Félez Muñoz*" (209). For the most part, however, the narrator directs his apostrophes to the reader to accentuate vividly a present state of affairs. Following are a few examples: "Llorando de los ojos, que non viestes atal" (l. 374) ["With tears flowing from their eyes, more than you have ever seen"], "veriedes armarse moros" (l. 697) ["you could see the Moors arming themselves"], "sabet, el otro" (l. 768) {"(I want you to) know that the latter"}, "Oíd qué dixo Minaya Álbar Fáñez" (l. 1127) {"Listen to what Minaya Álvar Fáñez said"}, "mala sobrevienta sabed que les cuntió" (l. 2281) {"a sudden bad incident, I want you to know, occurred to them}, "Aqueste era el rey Bucar si l'oviestes contar" (l. 2314) ["This was the Emir Búcar; perhaps you have heard tell of him"].[5]

Characters in the Cantar de Mio Cid

The *Cantar de Mio Cid* contains four major actants. The first is King Alfonso who banishes Rodrigo Díaz of Vivar, the Cid, from his realm, and thus sets into motion the events that will subsequently unfold in the epic poem. Another is the Cid, who must live by his wits and his military prowess to survive and satisfy the daily material needs of his fellow combatants, and who, in his subsequent conquest of the city of Valencia, rises to the socio-political level of a sovereign. The third major figure is Minaya Álvar Fáñez, the Cid's nephew, who is a chief military strategist in the Cid's entourage and, the Cid's ambassador of goodwill before King Alfonso in the Cid's numerous attempts to regain his monarch's favor. Finally, there are the infantes of Carrión, don Fernando and don Diego, conceivably the most villainous set of diegetic individuals depicted in Hispanic literature. Driven by their passion of greed, they marry the Cid's daughters solely to improve their economic lot and at the close of the epic poem they face a court of their noble peers to account for their subsequent immoral comportment toward their respective wives.

Among the minor characters in the epic poem, one must distinguish, on the one hand, between those who play an active, purposeful, and constructive structural role and, on the other, those who assume a passive stance. Among the former are Raquel and Vidas, Jewish businessmen who provide the Cid with the necessary monetary funds with which he defrays his immediate and urgent economic expenditures. Among the latter are the Cid's wife and his two daughters, recipients of actions enacted by others. Other secondary characters, such as don Ramón Berenguer, the count of Barcelona, and the Arab kings, simply serve as foils to highlight the Cid's military prowess and superiority over his enemies.

Analytical Study Objectives

This study attempts to decipher the composite morphological structure of the *Cantar de Mio Cid*. Chapter 2 reveals the number of tales that constitute the complex body of the *Cantar de Mio Cid*, which, to the best of my knowledge, has escaped critical attention of the poem's scholars. The subsequent three chapters detail the intrinsic, syntagmatic structure of the central core tales of the *Cantar de Mio Cid*. (The secondary tales, gyrating around the core tales, appear in the Appendix.) Moreover, throughout these chapters I endeavor to delve into the stylistic analysis of selective passages of the tales. Chapter 6, in turn, brings this study to a close by tying the structural analysis of the tales in the *Cantar de Mio Cid* to Propp's *Morphology of the Folktale* and by broaching the question regarding the general or universal validity of Propp's findings as they relate to the diegetic structures of complex literary works of art.

Chapter 2. The Number of Tales in the *Cantar de Mio Cid*

An analysis of the *Cantar de Mio Cid* reveals the existence of a minimum of four tales, if perceived solely from the perspective of the main character Rodrigo Díaz of Vivar, the Cid. The first tale would focus on don Rodrigo's exile and the travails he encounters within Moorish territories outside the realm of King Alfonso, including his conquests and subsequent defense of Moorish lands. The second tale deals with don Rodrigo's failed attempts to regain the good graces of his monarch, to whom he is constant in his loyalty, in the first part of the *Cantar de Mio Cid*. The third tale centers on the Cid's desire to be reunited with his family. The fourth tale deals with the Cid's need to marry off his daughters, doña Elvira and doña Sol. This approach, based exclusively on don Rodrigo's existential predicament, is unsatisfactory. To complete the structural fabric of the *Cantar de Mio Cid*, it is necessary to include the tales of the other participants in the epic poem, such as those of don Rodrigo's wife, doña Jimena; don Rodrigo's daughters, doña Elvira and doña Sol; Raquel and Vidas; and the vanquished Moors.

In this more comprehensive light, the composite morphologic rendition of the *Cantar de Mio Cid* reveals the existence of a minimum of nineteen tales. These tales and their titles are as follows:

Tale 1. The Tale of the Exile of Rodrigo Díaz, the Cid
Tale 2. The Tale of Doña Jimena, the Wife of Rodrigo Díaz
Tale 3. The Tale of Doña Elvira and Doña Sol, the Daughters of Doña Jimena and Rodrigo Díaz
Tale 4. The King of Valencia's Counterattack against the Cid
Tale 5. Gestures by the Cid to Regain the Good Will of King Alfonso
Tale 6. The Failure of Ramón Berenguer, Count of Barcelona, to Regain Lands Lost to the Cid
Tale 7. The Reaction of the Residents of Valencia against the Cid
Tale 8. The Failure of the King of Seville to Retake Valencia
Tale 9. The Tale of Raquel and Vidas
Tale 10. The Failure of King Yúsuf of Morocco to Recapture Valencia

Tale 11. The Tale of Fernando González and Diego González, the Infantes of Carrión

Tale 12. The Tale of the Cid's Handling of the Loose Lion Incident

Tale 13. The Tale of the Cid's Victory over the Moroccan King Búcar

Tale 14. The Tale of the Attempt by the Moroccan King Bucár to Reconquer Valencia

Tale 15. The Tale of the Moor Abengalbón's Encounter with the Infantes of Carrión

Tale 16. The Tale of the Revenge of the Cid on the Infantes of Carrión and the Remarriage of Doña Elvira and Doña Sol to the Infante of Navarre and Infante of Aragón

Tale 17. The Tale of King Alfonso

Tale 18. The Tale of the Infante of Navarre

Tale 19. The Tale of the Infante of Aragón

To present these tales in their chronological order throughout this study would unnecessarily clutter, complicate, and, possibly, muddle the reading of the literary events in question. Hence, I shall focus on the three core diegetic episodes that comprise the substance of the epic poem: Tale 1, The Tale of the Exile of Rodrigo Díaz, the Cid; Tale 11, The Tale of Don Fernando and Don Diego, the Infantes of Carrión; and Tale 16, The Tale of the Revenge of the Cid on the Infantes of Carrión. I analyze the other tales in the Appendix as they correlate to the above three main stories.

Chapter 3. The Tale of the Exile of Rodrigo Díaz, the Cid

The first tale of the *Cantar de Mio Cid* deals with the exile of the Cid. This narrative consists of sixteen moves and covers the Cid's travails and exploits in Spanish territories under Moorish rule, his conquest of Valencia, and his full pardon from King Alfonso.

Move 1 (Cantar I)
The first move is tacit. The initial verses that deal with the events leading to the Cid's falling out of favor with King Alfonso and the king's decree banishing don Rodrigo from his realm are missing. In his edition of the Poema de Mio Cid, Ramón Menéndez Pidal recreates what below constitutes the first move of the epic poem from the Crónica de Veinte Reyes and presents his prose summary of said pertinent events as the opening segment of the "Cantar primero. Destierro del Cid" (1966, 92–102).[1] Following is a symbolic transcription of Menéndez Pidal's intercalated segment-summary. The use of braces { } throughout this study indicates that the functions referred to are tacit.

$$\{\alpha\beta\gamma\delta A^{19}C\uparrow G^2H^1I^1K^4\downarrow\text{:o-LMN-ExU}\}$$

(The above symbolic transcription corresponds to the numerical functions: {I, II, III, VIII, X, XI, XV, XVI, XVIII, XIX, XX, XXIII, XXIV, XXV, XXVI, XXVIII, and XXX}.)

The initial situation {α} mentions that don Rodrigo, the Cid, is in Seville collecting the tribute that the Moorish King Motámid owes King Alfonso. At the same time, Abdállah Modáffar, the king of Granada, and Count García Ordóñez, a Christian in his service, prepare to wage war on the king of Seville. The initial scene continues with the absentation (function I: {β}) of King Abdállah Modáffar and his supporters from Granada and their march to Seville. It is at this point that the Cid receives information about the march and writes letters to King Abdállah Modáffar asking that Modáffar abandon his bellicose project (function II: interdiction {γ}), an interdiction that goes unheeded (function III: violation {δ}). The summary from the chronicle omits the next four immediate functions: function IV: reconnaissance [ε], in which the villain endeavors to obtain specific information regarding his victim; function V: delivery [ζ], by which the victim communicates pertinent data to his enemy; function VI: trickery [η], where the villain attempts to deceive his victim; and function VII: complicity [θ], whereby the victim, falling prey to the villain's act of deception, assists the villain in his perfidious intent. These omitted functions do not subsequently reappear in Move 1.

In the chronicle summary, the function that next appears after function III: violation is that of villainy (function VIII: {A}). King Abdállah Modáffar and his Christian allies declare war against King Motámid of Seville {A^{19}}. Upon learning that the king of Granada has declared war on the king of Seville, and has started his march (function IX: mediation, the connective incident {B}), don Rodrigo contracts to defend King Motámid (function X: beginning counteraction {C}). The Cid now leaves Seville (function XI: departure {↑}) and journeys to Cabra, where the villainous forces have established a foothold. The next three functions are absent—function XII: the first function of the donor [D]; function XIII: the hero's reaction [E]; and function XIV: provision or receipt of a magical agent [F]. The chronicle continues with Function XV: spatial transference between two kingdoms {G}, designating the Cid's arrival by land and on horseback at the immediate environs of the Castle of Cabra {G^2}. The chronicle then summarizes the outcome of the battle in an open field between the two opposing armies (function XVI: struggle {H^1}). Without describing any bodily injury to the hero (function XVII: branding, marking [J]), the chronicle proceeds to declare the army of don Rodrigo victorious (function XVIII: victory {I^1}), which resolves the initial bellicose provocation enacted by the king of Granada (function XIX: the initial misfortune or lack is liquidated {K^4}). Subsequently, the Cid goes back to Seville (function XX: return {↓}); he hands over his booty to King Motámid; he returns {↓} to the court of King Alfonso, the latter action marks a reversal of function XXIII: unrecognized arrival {o}; and he delivers the tribute of the king of Seville to his monarch. (Function XXI: pursuit, chase [Pr] and function XXII: rescue [Rs], do not appear in the chronicle summary, since they are irrelevant.) In the interim, don Rodrigo's enemies, who had intervened on behalf of the king of Granada, have raised false claims against the Cid (function XXIV: unfounded claims {L}). King Alfonso forces the Cid to confront (function XXV:

difficult task [M]) and resolve these claims (function XXVI: solution [N]), an assignment {M} that don Rodrigo fails to fulfill ({N-}). Function XXVII: recognition [Q] is of no import, since don Rodrigo is well known in the court, and thus this is another absent function. The following function is XXVIII: exposure [Ex], namely, that of the false hero or villain, which, from the point of view of don Alfonso, applies to the Cid {Ex}. Function XXIX: transfiguration [T], in which the hero's appearance in some positive way undergoes a change—that is, the hero receives or puts on new clothing, or he builds a new house—is inapplicable to the Cid. The chronicle summary continues with function XXX: punishment [U], as the king declares the Cid a persona non grata and exiles him from his lands {U}.[2] With function XXX and the epic text signaling the Cid's departure from his home in Vivar en route to Burgos, the first move of The Tale of the Exile of Rodrigo Díaz, the Cid closes. The last of the functions that Propp gives, namely, function XXXI: wedding [W], by which the hero acquires a bride or an appropriate, significant final award for duties performed, clearly has no place in Move 1.

Having analyzed in some detail the morphologic-syntagmatic structure of Move 1, I shall henceforth proceed to delineate in a schematic manner the morphological structures of the remaining moves of The Tale of the Exile of Rodrigo Díaz, the Cid.

Move 2 (Cantar I)

This Move broaches the Cid's need to find an intermediate safe haven as he endeavors to abandon Castile within the king's designated temporal deadline of nine days. The symbolic transcription of Move 2 follows:

$$a^5\S:B:^{4,2}C\uparrow\{D^2\}D^5E^5F:^9LMNw:^o\{K^4\}$$

(The above symbolic transcription corresponds to the numerical functions: VIIIa, IX, X, XI, {XII}, XII, XIII, XIV, XXIV, XXV, XXVI, and XXXI {XIX}.)[3]

Move 2 finds the Cid, with an entourage of sixty men, lacking lodging and food. He lacks, also, funds in general, since don Alfonso has confiscated his lands and other economic instruments. Destitute (a^5), the Cid begins his journey en route toward Burgos. (Leaving Vivar, the Cid and his men notice a crow to their right, a signal that foreshadows don

Rodrigo's triumph over the Moors during his years he will spend in exile; entering Burgos, don Rodrigo and his entourage espy a crow positioned to their left, an omen that constitutes a connective passage (§), one that foreshadows an immediate negative proleptic outcome.[4]) In a pseudo-scenic manner the narrator stresses that the residents of Burgos commiserate with the Cid. Their heartfelt sadness is evident:

> Burgeses e burgesas   por las finiestras son,
> plorando de los ojos,   tanto avién el dolor,
> de las sus bocas todos   dizían una razón:
> "—¡Dios, qué buen vassallo,   si oviesse buen
>   señor!—"   (ll. 17–20)
> {Men from the burgh and women from the burgh are
>   at the windows
> with tears streaming from their eyes, such pain they
>   had,
> from their mouths everyone one statement made:
> "God, what a good vassal, if he only had a good
>   lord"}

(The parelcon reference—the superfluous addition of "ojos" to the word "plorando"—indirectly serves to underscore the Cid's affective state as it is a repetitio of the same parelcon that the narrator used to characterize the Cid as he commenced his emigration from Castile: "De los sos ojos   tan fuertemientre llorando" (l. 1) {"From his eyes so strongly crying"}.[5]) The intrusive narrator immediately alerts the reader to the etiology behind the residents' reluctance to offer the Cid the courtesy that should be extended to a passing guest (B[4]), namely, that they had received an edict from King Alfonso prohibiting them from bestowing any kindness or comfort to don Rodrigo:

> Conbidarle ien de grado,   mas ninguno non osava:
> el rey don Alfonso   tanto avié la grand saña.
> Antes de la noche,   en Burgos d'él entró su carta
> con grand recabdo   e fuertemientre sellada:
> que a mio Cid Ruy Díaz   que nadi no l' diessen
>   posada,

> e aquel que ge la diesse   sopiesse vera palabra,
> que perderié los averes   e más los ojos de la cara,
> e aun demás   los cuerpos e las almas. (ll. 21–28)
> {They would have invited him with pleasure, but
>   no one dared to do so;
> the king, don Alfonso, was in such great rage.
> The night before, his letter-decree arrived in Burgos,
> with great precaution and heavily sealed,
> that nobody give lodging to My Cid Ruy Díaz,
> and that whoever did so should be aware <of this>
>   true edict,
> that he would lose his possessions and even more
>   so his eyes from his face,
> and their bodies and their souls as well.}

Stylistically, the above passage is uneven. It contains a partial segment that is artistically successful and two incongruous semantic passages. The aesthetically expressive lines relate to the king's somber threat of the dire consequences that will befall the residents of Burgos were they to assist the Cid and rest on the narrator's use of the verb "perderié," a prozeugma governing "averes" and "ojos." The two aesthetically flawed fragments involve: (1) the ellipsis of the conjugated verbs "brought" and "was," governing the two adverbial complements of manner "con grand recabdo" and "fuertemientre sellada," respectively, that makes the conjugated verb "entró" function as an awkward prozeugma; and (2) the semantic inconsistency that results from a double syllepsis—that is, the lack of grammatical concordance between the singular subject "nadi" and the plural verb "diessen" and the incongruous linkage of a singular third person pronominal demonstrative "aquel" and its corresponding singular verb "perderié" to the grammatically incompatible direct objects "cuerpos" ("bodies") and "almas" ("souls").

Structurally, the narrator's above analepsis amounts to a fill-in passage of an immediate past event. It sets the scene, also, for the abrupt action that ensues. The four-part scene commences with a catacosmesis—that is, with references made in a descending manner—and terminates in a climax. The pragmatographia moves progressively. It starts with a medium shot of the Cid's horsemen, who belligerently clamor for service before an inn; it moves to a waist-high shot of the Cid, who separates himself from his men and maneuvers his horse toward the closed portal of the building; it continues with a close-up of the Cid's foot leaving the stirrup; and it concludes with an extreme close-up of a particular detail of the Cid's shoe (or boot), that is, to the toe of the shoe (or boot) as it points at and then forcefully kicks the closed door:

> Los de mio Cid   a altas vozes llaman,
> los de dentro   non les querién tornar palabra.
> Aguijó mio Cid,   a la puerta se llegava,
> sacó el pie del estribera,   una feridal' dava;
> non se abre la puerta,   ca bien era cerrada.
> (ll. 35–39)
>
> [My Cid's men called out in loud voices,
> but those within would not say a single word in answer.
> My Cid spurred on his horse, and approached the door;
> he took his foot from the stirrup; he kicked the door,
> but it would not open, for it was firmly closed.]

Responding to the noise, an anonymous girl of nine years of age appears and stands before the Cid. Assuming the role of spokesperson for the other residents of her burgh, she antithetically looks upward at him and addresses don Rodrigo, reiterating the king's admonition and threat of severe punishment against those who come to the aid of the Cid and his men (B^4). Whereas the child's angle in this scene connotes inferiority, in delivering her speech she symbolically speaks down to him and thus ironically assumes a psychological stance of superiority. The antithetical relationship noted above extends to other aspects that render this scene very poignant, indeed: an unarmed child confronts an armed knight; a composed child, whose discourse is both measured and rational, contrasts to the irrational bawl of don Rodrigo's frantic men. Her circumlocutory anamnesis, a variant repetitio of lines 21–28, constitutes both an expression of dicaeologia, in that it is a defense or an excuse reasonably presented to justify the conduct of the burghers of the city, and a deesis, in that it is a perlocutionary supplication that the Cid abandon Burgos immediately so as to not put its inhabitants in harm's way (B^2):

—¡Ya Campeador,   en buen ora cinxiestes
                                              espada!
El rey lo ha vedado,   anoch d'él entró su carta
con grant recabdo   e fuertemientre sellada.
Non vos osariemos   abrir nin coger por nada;
Si non, perderiemos   los averes e las casas,
e demás   los ojos de las caras.
Cid, en el nuestro mal   vós non ganades nada,
mas el Criador vos vala   con todas sus vertudes
                                              santas.— (ll. 41–48)
["O Battler, in a favoured hour you girded your
                                              sword!
The King has forbidden us to take you in; his decree
                                              arrived last night,
brought with great precaution and carrying a heavy
                                              seal.
Nothing could persuade us to open to you or admit
                                              you,
for if we did we would lose our possessions and our
                                              homes,
and our eyes {from our faces} as well.
Cid, by our misfortune you gain nothing;
but may the Creator assist you with all his sacred
                                              power!"]

Heeding the child's advice, don Rodrigo retreats from Burgos (C). At the outskirts of the city (↑), the Cid encounters Martín Antolínez, a variant of a Christ figure who, as a donor (the function: $\{D^2\}$, is tacit), miraculously manages, somehow, to provide the Cid and his entire entourage with foodstuffs and wine ([F^4 var.]; Matt. 14:13–21; Luke 6:13–44; John 6:5–12). Stylistically, note the following examples of a prozeugma ("abástales") in conjunction with an isocolon ("de pan" and "de vino"):

> Martín Antolínez,   el burgalés conplido,
> a mio Cid e a los suyos   abástales de pan e de
> vino;
> non lo conpra,   ca él se lo avié consigo,
> de todo conducho   bien los ovo bastidos.
> (ll. 65–68)
> [Martín Antolínez, worthy citizen of Burgos,
> supplied My Cid and his men with bread and wine;
> he did not buy these, as he had his own supply;
> he had given them good provision of all the food
> they needed.]

Martín Antolínez, certain that King Alfonso will seek retribution against him for the act that he has just committed, assumes once more the role of a donor; this time he tests the Cid by turning into a suppliant. He requests that the Cid allow him to join his retinue(D^5). He expresses his state of angst by means of an opening antithetical plea: ("yagamos" / "váimosnos") and his confidence in a positive proleptic resolution of his present predicament by means of an alloiosis ("sano o bivo," / "cerca o tarde"):

> —Esta noch yagamos   e váimosnos al matino,
> ca acusado seré   por lo que vos he servido,
> en ira del rey Alfonso   yo seré metido.
> Si convusco escapo   sano o bivo,
> aun cerca o tarde el rey   quererm'á por amigo.—
> (ll. 72–76)
> ["Let us rest tonight and set off at dawn,
> for I shall be accused of having helped you,
> and incur the anger of King Alfonso.
> If I escape with you, alive and well,
> sooner or later the King will want meas his
> friend."]

Don Rodrigo, grateful to Martín Antolínez for his having liquidated an urgent present need, shows mercy to his supplicant and (metonymically) admits his "lança" into his group with an enthusiastic ecphonesis, stating that he will greatly recompense him at a later date (E^5): "—¡Martín Antolínez, sodes ardida lança, / si yo bivo, doblarvos he la soldada!—" (ll. 79–80) {"'Martín Antolínez, you are a courageous lance, / if I live I shall double your pay!'"}.

Made aware of the urgent economic needs that don Rodrigo faces, Martín Antolínez puts himself at the Cid's disposition (F^9) to act as an intermediary to negotiate a loan with the Jewish businessmen Raquel and Vidas in Burgos for two chests that the Cid plans to fill with sand. Note that the Cid, in effect, casts himself in the role of a false hero, a villain, whose proposed plan constitutes a deliberate act of fraud. Furthermore, in recruiting Martín Antolínez to assist him in his scheme, the Cid has become an evil counselor, converting Martín Antolínez into a co-conspirator and accessory in fraud (L).[6] Addressing Martín Antolínez, the Cid states:

—Espeso é el oro   e toda la plata,
bien lo vedes   que yo no trayo nada,
e huebos me serié   pora toda mi compaña.
Ferlo he amidos,   de grado non avrié nada:
con vuestro consejo   bastir quiero dos arcas,
inchámosla d'arena,   ca bien serán pesadas,
cubiertas de guadalmecí   e bien enclaveadas,
los guadamecís vermejos   e los clavos bien
                                        dorados.
Por Rachel e Vidas   vayádesme privado:
cuando en Burgos me vedaron conpra   e el rey me
                                        á airado,
non puedo traer el aver   ca mucho es pesado;
enpeñárgelo he   por lo que fuere guisado,
de noche lo lieven,   que non lo vean cristianos.—
                                        (ll. 81–93)
["I have spent the gold, and all the silver too;
as you can see very well, I bring nothing with me,
and I will need to pay my whole company;

what I propose, I shall do unwillingly; by choice I
                                     would take nothing.
With your help I want to prepare two chests;
let us fill them with sand, so they will be very heavy,
and cover them with embossed leather, finely
                                                studded:
bright red leather with brightly gilded studs.
Go quickly for me to Raquel and Vidas; tell them:
in Burgos I am forbidden to make purchases, and the
                                     King has exiled me;

I cannot take my valuables with me; they weigh too
                                                 much,
and so I will pledge them for a suitable sum;
let them be taken by night, that none shall see."]

Don Rodrigo, however, does not undertake this fraudulent act lightly. On the contrary, he is ridden with guilt because he commits a grave sin against his fellowmen, regardless of their race or religion. For example, the Cid has Moorish friends. A case in point is Abengalbón, a Moor who will subsequently accompany don Rodrigo's daughters, doña Elvira and doña Sol, and their husbands, the infantes of Carrión, from Molina to Ansarera. The residents of Castejón bless the Cid when he leaves their town because they are grateful to him for the humane manner in which he has treated them. As don Rodrigo adds, after recruiting Martín Antolínez as his partner in his crime of fraud against two other (innocent) individuals: "—Véalo el Criador   con todos los sos santos, / yo más non puedo   e amidos lo fago—" (ll. 94–95) ["'May the Creator, with all his saints, be my witness / that I can do no more, and that I act against my will'"].

Three lines later, Martín Antolínez is in Burgos, seeking out Raquel and Vidas—clearly a case of spatial and temporal foreshortening. When he finds them, a mimetic scene ensues in which the reader sees Martín Antolínez engaged in fulfilling the difficult task (M) that the Cid has requested he undertake, namely, to negotiate the terms for pawning the two chests of sand. The result is that Martín Antolínez deposits the two chests of sand with Raquel and Vidas as surety for the loan of a one-year period[7]; in return, he obtains six hundred marks of silver and gold, receiving, in turn, a commission for having brokered the transaction (N). The acquisition of these pecuniary funds resolves don Rodrigo's initial monetary difficulties (w^0) {K^4}. Note that the conversations between don Rodrigo and Martín Antolínez, between the latter and Raquel and Vidas, between don Rodrigo and the Jews, and between Raquel and Vidas constitute a doubling of segmental interludes.

Move 3 (Cantar I)
Move 3 deals with don Rodrigo's taking leave of his wife and two daughters. Following is the symbolic transcription of this move.

$$aC\uparrow:D^{2,7}E^2F:^9M:N$$

(The above symbolic transcription corresponds to the numerical functions: VIIIa, X, XI, XII, XIII, XIV, XXV, and XXVI.)[8]

The lack (a) refers to don Rodrigo separation from his wife, Jimena, and his two daughters, Elvira and Sol, for whom he has obtained a secure retreat at the monastery of Saint Peter of Cardeña during his exile. Hence, the Cid decides (C) to leave the environs of Burgos and sets out to visit with his family at the monastery ($\uparrow$). At the monastery, the abbot don Sancho, assuming the role of a donor, greets don Rodrigo and entreats him to remain as his guest ($D^{2,7}$): "—Gradéscolo a Dios, mio Cid   —dixo el abad don Sancho—, / pues aquí vos veo,   prendet de mí ospedado—" (ll. 246–47) ["'Thanks be to God, My Cid!'" said the abbot, Don Sancho, / 'Receive my hospitality, now you are come'"]. The Cid complies with the abbot's wishes (E^2): "Dixo el Cid: —Gracias, don abat,   e só vuestro pagado, / yo adobaré conducho   pora mí e pora mis vassallos; / mas, poque me vo de tierra,   dóvos cincuaenta marcos—" (ll. 248–50) ["The Cid said: 'Thank you, lord abbot; I am grateful to you. / I shall get ready provisions both for myself and for my vassals. / But, as I am going into exile, I give you fifty marks'"]. Don Rodrigo requests that don Sancho look after his family during his absence from Vivar: "— Dues fijas dexo niñas,   e prendetlas en los braços; / aquéllas vos acomiendo   a vós, abbat don Sancho, / d'ellas e de mi mugier   fagades todo recabdo—" (ll. 255–57) ["'I leave two young daughters; take them into your protection; / I commend them to you, abbot, Don Sancho; / take every care of them and of my wife'"]. The abbot, in turn, putting himself and the monastery at the

Cid's disposition (F⁹), readily grants don Rodrigo his wish: "Otorgado ge lo avié el abbat de grado" (l. 261) ["The abbot had granted it willingly"].

The scenes leading to the Cid's taking his leave of his family constitute a difficult task for don Rodrigo and are charged with pathos: exclamatory passages appear in the dialogue between husband and wife (ll. 266–84) and the Cid, holding his daughters in his arms, weeps and sighs, revealing his human condition: "a las sus fijas en braços las prendía, / llególas al coraçón, ca mucho las quería; / llora de los ojos, tan fuertemientre sospira" (ll. 275–77) {"he took his daughters in his arms / pressed them against his heart because he loved them so / he cries from his eyes and heaves heavy sighs"}. His departure (N) causes great pain, comparable to having one's nail stripped from one's finger: "Llorando de los ojos, que non viestes atal, / assís' parten unos d'otros commo la uña de la carne" (ll. 374–75) ["With tears flowing from their eyes, more than you have ever seen, / they parted, like the nail from the flesh"][9,10].

From a structural point of view, this episode contains two interesting scenic passages. At one point, the Cid, by means of an ecphonesis, expresses an optatio, one whose realization will not occur until the close of the epic poem: "—.Plega a Dios e a Santa María / que aún con mis manos case estas mis fijas!—" (ll. 282–82b) ["'May God and Saint Mary grant / that I myself may yet arrange marriages for these my daughters'"]. The other relates to two prayers that doña Jimena voices. The first, although exceedingly brief and offered simultaneous to the arrival of the Cid at the monastery, is a deesis that asks God to serve as her husband guide: "—Tú, que a todos guías, val a mio Cid el Canpeador—" (l. 241) ["'You who guide us all, support My Cid the Battler'"]. This prayer serves as a forerunner for doña Jimena's subsequent extensive prayer to Christ, in which she poses a difficult task (M) for Him by requesting that He safeguard her husband during his exile from the realm of King Alfonso.[11] Doña Jimena's second prayer, in turn, foreshadows the Cid's dream at a location called Navas de Palos. There, the archangel Gabriel assures him that he has nothing to fear during his lifetime and that the outcome of all his ventures will end well: "—bien se fará lo to—" (l. 409) ["'<while you live> all will go well for you'"].[12] The latter incident indicates the proleptic fulfillment of the difficult task (N) that doña Jimena had asked of Christ in her perlocutionary prayer at the dawn of her husband's departure from her side.

Move 4 (Cantar I)
In Move 4 the Cid and the men who accompany him leave the lands under the jurisdiction of King Alfonso. Below is the symbolic transcription of this move.

$$a^6B^3C{\uparrow}D^1E^1F^9G^2K^4$$

(The above symbolic transcription corresponds to the numerical functions: VIIIa, IX, X, XI, XII, XIII, XIV, XV, and XIX.)[13]

In a segmental interlude that foreshortens time and space, the Cid and his army traverse numerous geographic localities (Spinaz de Can, San Esteban, Ayllón, Alcubilla); they cross the Duero River at Navas de Palo and they rest at Figueruela. At the latter town don Rodrigo has a dream in which the angel Gabriel appears and assures him that he will fare well in his exile. Finally, they reach the Miedes Mountains with one day to spare before they must abandon the lands of King Alfonso (a). Like Moses, who takes a census of the Israelites at the request of God to gather the number of those who could be recruited as soldiers (Num. 1:2–3; Num. 26:2), so does don Rodrigo, in an interlude passage, attempt to gauge the strength of his cavalry, without taking into account the number in his infantry. (The parallel between the Cid and the mythical archetypal figure of Moses of the Hebrew Bible is a most interesting one, albeit, at first glance, ironic. Moses leads the Israelites toward their promised land and engages in warfare to secure his aim; don Rodrigo, as a leader of men, directs his people not to their cherished land of Castile, but away from it into a foreign, frightening environment. At this juncture, the Cid assumes a similar role as that played by the biblical warrior Joshua of Israel, for it is by force—that is, by continuously declaring war against the Moors—that don Rodrigo will lead his soldiers to a promised land, Valencia, where, following its conquest, he and his entourage will live in a paradisiacal environment, enjoying the waters of the sea, the sea air, and the agricultural products of an exceedingly fertile land. In view of the above, one can make a case that the creator of the *Cantar de Mio Cid* has provided his reader with a variant mythopoetic tale of the archetypal mythopoetic tale of Exodus as well as that of The Book of Joshua in the Hebrew Bible.) The result of the Cid's census reveals that he has three hundred horsemen under his command. The narrator renders the number of horsemen indirectly, by means of a metonymy: "sin las peonadas e omnes valientes que son, / notó trezientas lanças, que todas tienen pendones" (ll. 418–19) ["Not counting the foot soldiers, valiant as they were, / he reckoned three hundred lances, each with his pennant"].

While the size of the Cid's entourage is encouraging, it is, by the same token, a cause for some concern. The structural function of the Cid's census is to advert the reader that, once don Rodrigo enters enemy territory, he will not only have to engage aggressively in military actions of conquest, he, also, will continuously have to pillage the land. As the leader of a growing army, he must find the means by which to provide food supplies for his men every day as well as payment for their military service, a service that is either given on a fixed stipend or offered voluntarily.

To comply with the dictate of King Alfonso, the Cid prepares his retinue for the unpleasant moment of geographical transference and determines that they are to travel at night, a strategy that will help them avoid detection ($B^3C\uparrow$). The narrator summarizes their rite of passage in a single line that is an antithesis. This antithesis constitutes, also, a telescoping of space and a foreshortening of time: "De noch passan la sierra, vinida es la man" (l. 425) ["By night they crossed the mountains; the morning came"]. At this point, don Rodrigo assumes the role of a donor and tests his company of soldiers. He informs his men how he intends to proceed to obtain their reaction (D^1): "Díxoles a todos cómmo querié trasnochar" (l. 429) ["He told them all how he wanted to travel by night"]. Don Rodrigo's troops respond enthusiastically to his plan and, thereby, place themselves at his disposal (E^1F^9): "vassallos tan buenos por coraçón lo an, / mandado de so señor todo lo han a far" (ll. 430–31) ["[s]uch good vassals accepted willingly; / what their lord willed, all were to do"]. In the next five lines—lines that, again, constitute a spatial and temporal foreshortening—the Cid and his followers leave behind the lands of King Alfonso (G^2). With the latter, don Rodrigo liquidates the lack of this move (K^4), makes camp, and lies in wait to attack the town of Castejón:

Ante que anochesca piensan de cavalgar,
por tal lo faze mio Cid que no lo ventasse nadi;

andidieron de noch, que vagar non se dan.
O dizen Castejón, el que es sobre Fenares,
mio Cid se echó en celada con aquellos que él
trae. (ll. 432–36)
[Before nightfall they rode on their way,
My Cid acting thus to avoid discovery.
They travelled through the night; they gave
themselves no respite.
At the place known as Castejón, beside the river
Henares,
My Cid prepared an ambush with his followers.]

Move 5 (Cantar I)
The symbolic transcription of the narrative of the Cid's taking of Castejón follows:

$$a^{6,5}B:C\uparrow\{<\}H^1\{H^1\}I^1\{I^1\}K^4Nw:^o$$

(The above symbolic transcription corresponds to the numerical functions: VIIIa, IX, X, XI, XVI, XVIII, XIX, XXV, XXVI, and XXXI.)[13]

The Cid realizes that his location within Moorish territories is uncomfortably close to the lands of King Alfonso. Moreover, he has limited monetary funds: the reader will recall that the Cid has given a portion of the monies he received from Raquel and Vidas to the abbot of the monastery to cover lodging and other expenses of his family. Don Rodrigo needs, first, to place himself and his men at a safe distance from the forces of don Alfonso and, second, to acquire wealth ($a^{6,5}$). Like a lion stalking its prey, the Cid cannot afford to rest for long in his concealed position overlooking Castejón. If nothing else, he must provide provisions to his three hundred horsemen and to his foot soldiers. He must launch an attack against Castejón or begin to pillage the surrounding countryside or, perhaps, simultaneously do both. At the Cid's command post, Minaya Álvar Fáñez, whose passion to constantly engage the Moors in combat throughout the *Cantar de Mio Cid* will never wane, promptly calls on the Cid to plan a trap for the residents of Castejón. In turn, the Cid immediately presents his strategy to conquer Castejón, a conquest about which he avers all Spain will rave: "—¡d'aqueste acorro fablará toda España!—" (453) [All Spain shall talk of this deed"]. Stylistically, he highlights his discourse by his use of the polysyndeton, by employing assonant-paroxytone rhyme ("a-a," "i-a," "e-o," "o-a," "a-o"), by introducing alliteration (especially of the consonants: "l," "b," "g," "f," and "m"), and by instigating, exhorting his men, a deesis delivered in the imperative mood, that they be fearless and ruthless in their attack (BC):

  —Vós con los dozientos idvos en algara;
  allá vaya Álbar Álbarez e Álbar Salvadórez, sin
              falla,
  e Galín García, una fardida lança,
  cavalleros buenos que acompañen a Minaya.
  A osadas corred, que por miedo non dexedes
              nada,
  Fita ayuso e por Guadalfajara,
  fata Alcalá lleguen las algaras,
  e bien acojan todas las ganancias,
  que por miedo de los moros non dexen nada;
  e yo con los ciento aquí fincaré en la çaga,
  terné yo Castejón, don abremos grand enpara.
  Si cueta vos fuere alguna al algara,
  fazedme mandado muy privado a la çaga;
  ¡d'aqueste acorro fablará toda España!—
             (ll. 442–53)

["You, with two hundred men, make a raid.
Álvar Álvarez should go, and the matchless Álvar
            Salvadórez
and Galindo García, a brave warrior;
let the good knights accompany Minaya.
Attack courageously, and lose nothing through fear.
Down past Hita and Guadalajara,
as far as Alcalá let the raids extend;
they should make sure they take all the booty
and leave nothing for fear of the Moors.
And I shall stay here in the rear with my hundred
            men.

> I shall take Castejón, where we shall be well
> protected.
> If you should encounter any danger in the advance,
> send me word immediately to the rear.
> All Spain shall talk of this deed."]

A temporal foreshortening passage follows, which the intrusive narrator renders in an auxesis manner, revealing a delicate pictorial manipulation of light. The darkness of the night in which the above discourse unfolds now promptly gives way to Homer's "rosy fingers" of dawn, to the bright light of morning projected by a sun emerging from its journey through nocturnal lands. Note that even the intrusive creator ironically waxes poetically and enthusiastically over his succinctly created ecphrasis, introducing himself into the picture by means of a parenthetic ecphonesis that expresses his admiration of Nature's (of his) freshly painted canvas: "Ya quiebran los albores e vinié la mañana, / ixié el sol, ¡Dios, qué fermoso apuntava!" (ll. 456–57) ["Now dawn was breaking and the morning coming; / the sun rose, Lord God how beautiful it shone!"].

Early in this wondrous morning, Castejón comes alive. The omniscient narrator expresses the activity summarily in an auxesis enumeration governed by the figure diazeugma:

> En Castejón   todos se levantavan,
> abren las puertas,   de fuera salto davan,
> por ver sus lavores   e todas sus heredades.
> Todos son exidos,   las puertas abiertas an
> dexadas. (ll. 458–61)
> [The inhabitants of Castejón rose from their beds,
> opened the gates and went out
> to go about their labours and work their land.
> They had left, leaving gates open.]

With the majority of its inhabitants outside the protection of the city's wall: "las yentes de fuera   todas son derramadas" (l. 463) ["The people had all scattered outside the town"], the city becomes vulnerable to a military assault. It is at this point that the Cid dispatches this collective body of heroes from the campsite ({<}). With one hundred horsemen at his side, the Cid and his men gallop toward the gates of the town (↑). The attack takes the people of Castejón by surprise and his men take prisoners and pick up cattle as booty. Note the narrator's continued use of diazeugma and the rare appearance of a mesozeugma:

> El Campeador   salió de la celada,
> corrié   a Castejón sin falla,
> moros e moras   aviélos de ganancia,
> e essos gañados   cuantos en derredor andan.
>
> (ll. 464–66)
>
> [The Battler left his hiding place
> and fell at once upon Castejón.
> They captured Moorish men and women
> and took all the cattle near the town.]

While his men are busily engaged in gathering collectible items, the Cid, meanwhile, heads toward the town, causing those guarding the city's entrance door to abandon their post in panic. Of the Cid's action, the narrator presents to his reader a pragmatographia. The narrative depicts don Rodrigo—for the reader this must consist of an initial long-shot view—charging into the city with his sword raised. The reader then envisions the Cid in a shot from the waist up, and in the next view of don Rodrigo, the reader envisions in her / his mind's eye, a close-up of the arm and sword of the Cid flashing in semicircular swoops, mercilessly cutting down fifteen Moors who stand in his path. The use of an anastrophe, the placement of the adjective "desnuda" before the noun "espada," which in another context might very well be considered a parelcon, here serves to emphasize the terror that its presence produces among the few Moors remaining within the walls of Castejón. Thus, the narrator avers, does the silver-gold-rich town of Castejón fall to the arms of the Cid ($H^1I^1K^4w^o$):

> Mio Cid don Rodrigo   a la puerta adeliñava,
> los que la tienen,   cuando vieron la rebata,
> ovieron miedo,   e fue desenparada.
> Mio Cid Ruy Díaz   por las puertas entrava,
> en mano trae   desnuda el espada,

quinze moros matava   de los que alcançava;
gañó a Castejón   e el oro e la plata. (ll. 467-73)
[My Cid Don Rodrigo made straight for the gate;
those who guarded it, when they saw the attack,
took fright; it was left unprotected;
My Cid entered through the gate,
his sword unsheathed in his hand;
he killed fifteen Moors that he found in his path.
He took Castejón, and the gold and silver.]

    Synchronic to the actions just narrated of the Cid are those in which his nephew, Minaya Álvar Fáñez, and his fearless cavalry of over two hundred engage in the environs of Castejón. The forces of the Cid's nephew plunder the towns in the vicinity of Castejón up to Alcalá—the narrator states as much and chooses not to narrate any of the particular scenes of their military engagement ($\{<H^1I^1\}$). What the narrator does indulge in, however, is a description of the booty that Minaya Álvar Fáñez and his marauders bring back to Castejón (w^o):

Fasta Alcalá llegó   la seña de Minaya
e desí arriba   tórnanse con la ganancia,
Fenares arriba   e por Guadalfajara.
Tanto traen   las grandes ganancias,
muchos gañados   de ovejas e de vacas,
e de ropas,   e de otras riquizas largas.
(ll. 477b–81b)
[... Minaya's ensign reached Alcalá,
and from that point they returned with their booty
up the Henares valley past Guadalajara.
They brought back such great wealth;
many cattle and flocks of sheep,
clothing and other riches.]

    Segmented interludes are created by the closing scenes that present a conversation between the Cid and his nephew, Minaya Álvar Fáñez, and the subsequent distribution of the booty they have acquired. Finally, the victory with its booty, only partially liquidates the initial lack of Move 4 (K^4). Still in harm's way—close enough for the forces of don Alfonso can attack him and inflict serious losses on his men—the Cid decides not to keep any prisoners. Instead, he puts them up for sale, which amounts to a difficult task (M). (Don Rodrigo exempts two hundred Moorish men and women, whom he sets free so that the Moors will not condemn him: "—que de mí non digan mal—" (l. 535) ["'that they shall not speak ill of me'"].) With the sale of the remaining residents of Castejón to the Moors of Hita and Guadalajara for three thousand marks of silver, don Rodrigo resolves his difficult task (Nw^o) and departs from Castejón without razing the town or executing its residents. For his humane comportment, the Cid egresses from Castejón with its inhabitants blessing him: "Los moros e las moras   bendiziéndol' están" (l. 541) ["They were blessed by the Moors"].

Move 6 (Cantar I)
The symbolic transcription of the narrative of the Cid's taking of Alcocer follows:

$$aBC{\uparrow}H{:}^1 \; I{:}^1 {\downarrow} K^4$$

(The above symbolic transcription corresponds to the numerical functions: VIIIa, IX, X, XI, XVI, XVIII, XX, and XIX.)[13]
The Cid's arrival at the outskirts of Alcocer in the province of Aragon, lands dependent on the Moorish King Tamín, occurs in record time in a passage that clearly represents a telescoping of space and a foreshortening of time. In twelve lines the narrator informs his reader that don Rodrigo traverses and plunders Henares, Alcarria, Anguita, Taranz; that he pitches camp between Fariza and Cetina; and that he passes through Alhama, La Foz, Bubierca, and Ateca. The above constitutes an introductory interlude.

On a rugged hill overlooking Alcocer, the Cid and his men dig in with the stated purpose, according to the narrator, of avoiding a surprise counterattack: "a todos sos varones   mandó fazer una cárcava, / que de día nin de noch   non les diessen arrebata, / que sopiessen que mio Cid allí avié fincança" (ll. 561–63) ["<The Battler> ordered that . . . / all his men should dig a defensive ditch / so that no surprise attack could be made on them by day or by night / and that it should be known that My Cid had come to stay"]. At this point, the narrator emphasizes to his reader, by his stylistic use of a variant of an anaphora, a prozeugma, an isocolon, a polysyndeton, and an apostrophe to the reader, that the entire region is aware of the Cid's exploits in Moorish lands and that many towns and villages, indeed, now pay material tribute ("parias") to the Cid: "Los de Alcocer   a mio Cid ya'l' dan parias, / e los de Teca   e los de Terrer la casa. / A los de Calataút,   sabet, mal les pesava" (ll. 570–72) ["The inhabitants of Alcocer paid tribute willingly, / and so too did the inhabitants of Ateca and of the town of Terrer. / Those of Calatayud, I tell you, were deeply worried."].

Next, in a line that denotes a temporal foreshortening, the narrator explicitly states that the Cid has spent the last fifteen weeks lying in wait: "Allí yogo mio Cid   complidas quinze semanas" (l. 573) ["My Cid stayed there for a full fifteen weeks"], without those in Alcocer willing to capitulate (a). The Cid proposes to seize the city by means of a ruse: they will pretend to retreat and then will turn back and attack the Moors when the residents of Alcocer evacuate their city to pursue them (BC↑):

> Cuando vio mio Cid   que Alcocer non se le dava,
> él fizo un art   e non lo detardava:
> dexa una tienda fita   e las otras levava,
> cojós' Salón ayuso,   la su seña alçada,
> las lorigas vestidas   e cintas las espadas,
> a guisa de menbrado,   por sacarlos a celada.
> (ll. 574–79)
>
> [When My Cid saw that Alcocer did not yield to him,
> he at once prepared to trick its people:
> he struck camp but left one tent standing,
> and moved off down the Jalón, with his standard raised,
> his men wearing their armour and with swords girded on;
> with cunning, he aimed to draw his enemies into a trap.]

The stratagem works. As the Cid had foreseen, the residents abandon Alcocer in pursuit of the supposedly retreating Spaniards:

> Veyénlo los de Alcocer, ¡Dios, cómmo se alabavan!:
> —Fallido á a mio Cid el pan e la cevada;
> las otras abés lieva, una tienda á dexada;
> de guisa va mio Cid commo si escapasse de arrancada.
> Demos salto a él e feremos grant ganancia,
> antes que'l' prendan los de Terrer, si non, non nos darán dent nada;
> la paria qu'él á presa tornárnosla ha doblada.—
> Salieron de Alcocer a una priessa much estraña.
> (ll. 580–87)
> [The inhabitants of Alcocer saw this. Lord God, how they boasted!
> "My Cid has run out of bread and fodder;
> he can hardly manage his tents; he has left one behind;
> My Cid is leaving as if he were fleeing from a rout.
> Let us attack him and bring back great booty,
> before it is taken by the men of Terrer.
> If we do not, nothing will be left for us.
> He will give us back twice the tribute he has taken!"
> In great haste, they rushed out from Alcocer.]

    At this point, the Cid orders his men to counterattack and engage the Moors in direct combat in an open field (H^1): "—¡Firidlos, cavalleros, todos sines dubdança! / ¡Con la merced del Criador, nuestra es la ganancia!—" (ll. 597–98) ["'Strike fearlessly, my knights / with the help of the Creator, the gain is ours!'"]. Seven lines following his above ecphonesis and paratactic pronouncement, the Cid's troops, in the span of just over one hour, slay three hundred Moors and defeat their enemy (I^1). The hyperbole below involves a foreshortening of time: "Los vassallos de mio Cid sin piedad les davan, / en un ora e un poco de logar trezientos moros matan" (ll. 604–5) ["My Cid's vassals attacked the Moors mercilessly, / and in little over an hour they had killed three hundred"].

    A comment with respect to the combat over Alcocer and its aftermath is in order. Interestingly, the battle scene is not vividly developed along the lines of action. The passage is memorable, in the main, for its poetic emphasis of interior rhyme. (This passage includes, also, alliteration in many of these same lines; two apostrophes to the reader: "tienen buenos cavallos,   sabet, a su guisa les andan (l. 602) ["[t]hey had good horses, I tell you, which obeyed them willingly"] and "Mio Cid gañó a Alcocer,   sabet, por esta maña" (l. 610) ["By this trick, I tell you, My Cid won Alcocer"]; an ellipsis tied to an isocolon: "—¡Grado a Dios del cielo   e a todos los sos santos!—" (l. 614) ["'Thanks be to God in heaven and to all his saints!'"]; and a polyptoton: "los moros e las moras" (l. 619) {"Moorish men and Moorish women"}.) I take the examples of interior rhyme that follow from lines 570–622. In the samples I cite below, I present only those instances in which the interior rhyme, for the most part assonant, occurs in the same line or in consecutive lines. There is one case of an assonant-oxytone rhyme of an acute "e": "Mio Cid gañó a Alcocer   sabet, por esta maña." There are numerous instances of the assonant-paroxytone rhyme of "e-a": "dexa una tienda fita   e las otras levava, / cojós' Salón ayuso,   la su seña alçada"; "—las otras abés lieva,   una tienda á dexada—"; "—la paria qu'él á presa   tornárnosla ha doblada. —/ Salieron de Alcocer   a una priessa much estraña"; "abiertas dexan las puertas,   que ninguno non las guarda" (l. 593) ["they left the gates open and unguarded"]; "mandó tornar la seña,   apriessa espoloneavan" (l. 596) ["He ordered the ensign to turn back and they spurred on at a great pace"]. Following are four instances in two lines of an assonant-paroxytone rhyme of "i-a": "las lorigas vestidas   e cintas las espadas, / a gisa de menbrado." Below are two cases of the paroxytone rhyme of "o-o": "en un ora e un poco de logar   trezientos moros matan" and "metióla en somo,   en todo lo más alto" (l. 612) ["and placed it <the standard> on the very highest point"]. There is one instance of a consonant-paroxytone rhyme of "ando": "Dando grandes alaridos   los que están en la celada, / dexando van los delant,   por el castiello se tornavan" (ll. 606–7) ["Caught in the trap, the Moors shrieked loudly / as the Cid, with his small band, spurred on towards the fortress"]. There are, also, two lines that stress the interior rhyme of the final acute vowel "'o": "Mio Cid, cuando los vio fuera,   cogiós' commo de arrancada, / cojós' Salón ayuso,   con los sos abuelta anda" (ll. 588–89) ["My Cid, seeing them outside the town, rode off as though fleeing from the field. / Down the Jalón he went, together with his men"].

Finally, the paroxytone rhyme of "e-o"—in both consonant and assonant rhymed patterns—is the most prevalent: "—Demos salto a él e feremos grant ganancia—"; "vio que entr'ellos e el castiello mucho avié grand plaça" (l. 595) ["<he> saw the great distance between them and the citadel"]; "Bueltos son con ellos por medio de la llana, / ¡Dios, qué bueno es el gozo por aquesta mañana!" (ll. 599–600) ["They fell to battle in the middle of the plain. / Lord God, how great was the joy on that morning!"]; "tienen buenos cavallos, sabet, a su guisa les andan, / entr'ellos e el castiello en essora entravan" (ll. 602–3) ["They had good horses, I tell you, which obeyed them willingly. / Now they passed between the Moors and the fortress"]. And, lastly, the following passage has an overabundance of paroxytone rhyme of "e-o" in both consonant and assonant form:

   —¡Grado a Dios del cielo e a todos los sos santos,
   ya mejoraremos posadas a dueños e a cavallos!
   Oíd a mí, Álbar Fáñez e todos los cavalleros:
   en este castiello grand aver avemos preso,
   los moros yazen muertos, de bivos pocos veo;
   los moros e las moras vender non los podremos,
   que los descabecemos nada non ganaremos,
   cojámoslos de dentro, ca el señorío tenemos,
   posaremos en sus casas e d'ellos nos serviremos.
           — (ll. 614–22)

["Thanks be to God in heaven and to all his saints!
Now riders and horses shall have a better resting place.
Listen to me, Álvar Fáñez, and all my knights!
In this fortress we have gained much booty;
the Moors lie dead, I see a few alive.
We shall be unable to sell the Moors as slaves, neither men nor women;
we should gain nothing by beheading them.
Let us bring them in, for we are the lords;
we shall stay in their homes and use them as our servants."]

With his victory over the Moors, the Cid enters unimpeded through the gates of Alcocer; he takes possession of the city ($\downarrow$); and he subjugates the remaining sparse population to serve the daily needs of his men. The conquest of Alcocer liquidates the Cid's lack in two ways: it places Alcocer under the Cid's control, and it puts the Cid and his army out of reach of the king of Castile. At this point of the diegesis the Cid is both powerful and safe from King Alfonso's retaliation (K^4).

Move 7 (Cantar I)
This move entails don Rodrigo's defense of Alcocer from a counterattack launched by the forces of King Tamín of Valencia. The symbolic transcription of Move 7 follows:

$$A^{19}BC\uparrow\S H:^1 I:^1 K^4 \downarrow w^o:$$

(The above symbolic transcription corresponds to the numerical functions: VIII, IX, X, XI, XVI, XVIII, XIX, XX, and XXXI.)[14]

The vassals of King Tamín reside in the surrounding areas of Alcocer. They convince the king of Valencia that the continued presence of the Cid poses a serious proleptic threat to his authority and possessions, and, consequently, the king unhesitatingly declares war on don Rodrigo (A^{19}). The king's army of three thousand men, under the command of King Fáriz and King Galve, blockade the city of Alcocer for three weeks. As elsewhere, the narrator here chooses to foreshorten time: "toviérongela en cerca   complidas tres semanas" (l. 664) ["The siege lasted a full three weeks"]. The blockade exhausts don Rodrigo's rations and water supply and forces him to deliberate on his next action. In the following anacoenosis, the Cid democratically solicits advice from his knights: "—Dezidme, cavalleros,   cómmo vos plaze de far—" (l. 670) ["'Tell me, my knights, what you think we should do!'"]. As usual, Minaya Álvar Fáñez is the first—and here, the last—to speak up. He urges the Battler to engage the enemy immediately. His world view is one of power politics: The Spaniards must engage in war. If the Moors defeat them, they will disappear from life's stage; if they are victorious, they will impose their will upon the Moorish people of Spain. In Moorish lands, where the population is inhospitable to the Cid's men, they must not bewail their existential plight, but constantly choose to fight and survive. For Minaya Álvar Fáñez, whose existential view of life is aligned with pragmatism, the choice comes down to the following: to do or die. The Moorish forces vastly outnumber the Spaniards at six to one, a situation of dramatic irony given that the reader knows more than the Spaniards do about the actual number of men in the Moorish army. Minaya Álvar Fáñez advises don Rodrigo that the Spaniards should be the ones to initiate the attack (B):

> Primero fabló Minaya,   un cavallero de prestar:
> —De Castiella la gentil   exidos somos acá,
> si con moros non lidiáremos,   no nos darán del pan.
> Bien somos nós seiscientos,   algunos ay de más;
> en el nombre del Criador,   que non pase por ál:
> vayámoslos ferir   en aquel día de cras.—
> (ll. 671–76)
> [First to speak was Minaya, an excellent knight:
> "We have come to this place from our beloved Castile.
> If we do not fight with Moors we gain no bread.
> There are a good six hundred of us, indeed a few more.
> In the name of the Creator, let us take no other way but to attack them tomorrow!"]

The Cid shares Minaya Álvar Fáñez's view. Picking up on his nephew's words, don Rodrigo firmly avers that they will launch a counterattack (C): "Dixo el Campeador: —A mi guisa fablastes, / ondrástesvos, Minaya,   ca avérvoslo iedes de far—" (ll. 677–78) ["The Battler spoke: 'What you have said is to my liking. / You have brought honour on yourself Minaya, which I would have expected of you'"]. The eviction of the residents of Alcocer from the city as a measure to maintain the secrecy of their plans of engagement is a segmental interlude: its erasure would not affect the main course of the action of Move 7.

The encounter about to ensue is of capital importance. The two previous conflicts were skirmishes: the Cid's forces had taken on local militia, not professional soldiers. In reality, the military mettle of the Cid and his retinue remains as yet untested. Don Rodrigo shows he is aware of this fact when he addresses his troops before dawn on the following day. For the Cid, as for Minaya Álvar Fáñez, this military engagement will be their moment of truth. As the light of dawn begins to break over the eastern horizon, the Battler addresses his trusted cavalry:

—Todos iscamos fuera,   que nadi non raste,
sinon dos peones solos   por la puerta guardar.
Si nós muriéremos en campo,   en castiello nos
                                                entrarán;
si venciéremos la batalla,   creçremos en rictad.—
(ll. 685–88)
["Let us all go forth and none remain behind
save two footsoldiers to guard the gate.
If we die on the field of battle, the Moors will take
                                        the fortress;
and if we win the battle, we shall gain yet more
                                            wealth."]

The Cid and his army cross the doors of the city (↑). To highlight the significance of this engagement, the narrator presents several passages that connect (§) the function of departure (↑) to that of struggle (H)—that is, of the engagement of the two forces in direct combat. These passages offer a pragmatographia that will linger in the mind's eye of the reader long after the reading of this diegetic event has transpired.

The unexpected appearance of the Cid's army causes confusion among the Moorish sentinels who, caught by surprise, hasten back to their camp to report the event. The narrator's ecphonetic comment on the state of turmoil that reigns among the Moors reveals that not a single enemy soldier stands ready armed to fight: "¡Qué priessa va en los moros!   e tornáronse a armar" (l. 695) ["How the Moors rushed to rearm themselves!"]. What follows is a prosopopoeia in which the alliterative consonant sound of the drums, produced by the alveolar trill "rr," the alveolar "t," the velar "k," and bilabial "br," is so great that it can very well split the earth into splinters: "ante roído de atamores   la tierra querié quebrar" (l. 696) ["At the beating of the drums it seemed that the earth would break open"].

35

The Moors recover, organize, and commence their march against the Cid's men. Visually, the description constitutes a long-shot view. A narratorial erotesis underscores the enormous number of men in the Moorish army and creates a sense of tension for the fight that must immediately ensue: "De parte de los moros dos señas ha cabdales / e fizieron dos azes de pendones mezclados,   ¿quí los podrié contar? / Las azes de los moros   ya s' mueven adelant" (ll. 698–700) ["The Moors had two main standards / and formed two lines of mixed infantry. Who could count them? / Now the lines of the Moors moved ahead"]. Next, the narrator cuts back to the Cid and his forces, presenting both incidents as synchronic actions. The diegesis is highly cinematic—clearly, cinematography's use of montage constitutes a direct borrowing from literature. The Moorish army moves forward while the Cid and his men passively stand, immobile, attentively gazing at the advancing Moorish soldiers. There is a sense of tension among all. The Cid explicitly orders his men not to move until he orders otherwise: "—Quedas sed, mesnadas,   aquí en este logar, / non derranche ninguno   fata que yo lo mande—" (ll. 702–3) ["'Be still, my troops, do not move from here; / let none break ranks till I give the command'"].

Following this speech, the tension mounts. Hardly has the sound of the Cid's last words ceased when Pedro Bermúdez, a nephew of the Cid, is unable to withstand the tension any further. With the army's ensign in his hand, he begins to spur his horse's flank. Looking at the Cid as his mount stirs to life, he shouts: "—¡El Criador vos vala,   Cid Campeador leal! / Vo meter la vuestra seña   en aquella mayor az; / los que el debdo avedes   veremos cómmo la acorrades—" (ll. 706–8) ["'May the Creator protect you, Cid, O loyal Battler! / I am going to post your ensign in the main enemy line. / We shall see how you can protect it—those of you who are responsible!'"]. Ignoring Cid's ecphonetic deesis-optatio: "Dixo el Campeador: —¡Non sea, por caridad!—" (l. 709) ["The Battler shouted out: 'Do not go, for the love of mercy!'"], Pedro Bermúdez rushes headlong into the forces of the Moors—his act constitutes the initial instance of a struggle in an open field (H^1). A close-up of Pedro Bermúdez's entanglement with the Moors follows. Moorish soldiers render blows to Pedro Bermúdez, endeavoring unsuccessfully to knock him off his horse: "Moros le reciben   por la seña ganar, / danle grandes colpes,   mas no l' pueden falsar" (ll. 712–13) ["Moors rushed forward towards him to seize the ensign; / though they struck him heavy blows, they could not pierce his armour"]. Next, the narrator cuts back again to the Cid and offers a close-up of his face as he ecphonetically entreats his men to succor his valiant nephew: "Dixo el Campeador: ¡Valelde, por caridad!—" (l. 714) ["The Battler cried out: 'Help him, in love of mercy!'"].

The tension in this sequence keeps mounting. The Cid's men do not dash forward to enact their commander's order. Instead, the narrator chooses to stall the action and present, in a slide-show manner, how the Cid's cavalry prepare for action. He does so by employing conjugated verbs in the present tense of the indicative mood—"Enbraçan," "abaxan,"—a verb form that in narrative is typically reserved for commentary, by encasing the above verbs in a paratactic structure—as noted by De Chasca (205–6), the use of paratactic structure is not uncommon in this epic poem—and by enumerating the details of the preparation of don Rodrigo's cavalry through the use of the asyndeton: the horsemen secure their shields not to their chests, but to their "hearts;" they draw down their lances; finally, they lower their faces above their saddlebows. One would think that next they charge, but this is not the case. The narrator prolongs the tension with his use of the iteratio-ploce "coraçones." These men, the narrator tells his reader, as if he or she were ignorant of this fact, are valiant of heart, ready to strike the enemy with great courage. Note, moreover, that the narrator fixes his reader's attention to these paratactic lines, also, by his use of the assonant-paroxytone rhyme of "a-a" in lines 715–17, by the alliteration of the vowel "a"—a vowel that the narrator repeats sequentially seven times in line 716—by his use of the consonant-paroxytone ending rhyme of "ones", and by his use of the alliteration of the consonant "f" in line 718:

> Enbraçan los escudos   delant los coraçones,
> abaxan las lanças   abueltas de los pendones,
> enclinaron las caras   de suso de los arzones,
> ívanlos ferir   de fuertes coraçones." (ll. 715–18)
> [They clasped [*sic*] their shields before their hearts
> and lowered ; their lances with their pennants;
> they kept their heads low over the saddle-bow
> and advanced [*sic*] to strike them with strong hearts.]

At last, in an ecphonesis that is an augendi causa, as well, the Cid commands his men to charge the enemy. The structure of lines 720–21 is, also, paratactic: "A grandes vozes llama   el que en buen ora nació: / — ¡Feridlos, cavalleros,   por amor del Criador! / ¡Yo só Ruy Díaz,   el Cid Campeador!—" (ll. 719–21) ["The man born in a favoured hour cried out at the top of his voice: / 'Strike them, my knights, for the love of mercy! / I am Ruy Díaz the Cid, the Battler of Vivar!"]. The Cid's three hundred horsemen now enter the fray and converge where Pedro Bermúdez is struggling to survive. Hyperbole reigns supreme in the next combat scene in the open field (H^1). The Cid's soldiers kill six hundred Moors instantly:

>   Todos fieren en el az   do está Pero Vermúez,
>   trezientas lanças son,   todas tienen pendones;
>   seños moros mataron,   todos de seños colpes;
>   a la tornada que fazen   otros tantos son."
>   (ll. 722–25)
> [They all struck at the battle line, round Pedro
>   Bermúdez;
> there were three hundred lances, each with its
>   pennant;
> they killed as many Moors, with one blow each,
> and as many again in the next charge.]

Next, the narrator vividly renders, once again by his use of paratactic structure, a pictorial synthesis of the devastating battle: chromatic hues of white contrast sharply with those of crimson. The initial scene commences with the narrator addressing an apostrophe to his reader ("Veriedes"). He then recreates the turmoil of the battle by means of the trope metonymy—the instrument substitutes for the user of the same—and the figures antithesis ("premer e alçar"), anaphora and polyptoton ("tanta"/ "tanta"/ "tantos"), quincolon ("tantas lancas" / "tanta adágara"/ "tanta loriga" / "tantos pendones" / "tantos . . . cavallos"), and polysyndeton ("e"). In addition, the narrator keeps his reader's eyes fixed to his words by the deliberate repetition in lines 726–28 of the vowel "a," by the consonant-oxytone rhyme of infinitives in "ar" ("alçar" / "foradar" / "pasar" / "falsar" /

"desmanchar"), and by the use of the assonant-paroxytone rhymes of "a-o" and "e-o" in lines 729–30. (From the above lines, the reader will have noted that verbs appear in the infinitive form—that is, the narrator depicts this graphic and moving scene without providing his reader with a single conjugated verb.) Finally, a circumlocution indicates the innumerable Moorish horsemen killed in this battle. The narrator's bird's-eye view of the scene follows:

>Veriedes tantas lanças   premer e alçar,
>tanta adágara   foradar e pasar,
>tanta loriga   falsar e desmanchar,
>tantos pendones blancos   salir vermejos en sangre,
>tantos buenos cavallos   sin sos dueños andar.
>
>   (ll. 726–30)
>[You could see so many lances lowered and raised again,
>so many shields pierced right through,
>so much armour holed and torn,
>so many white pennants stained
>so many white pennants stained red wih blood,
>so many fine horses, wandering riderless.]

The Moors, in a prozeugma, clamor for assistance to "Mafómat" while Christians, in turn, antithetically call upon "Santi Yagüe": "Los moros llaman—¡Mafómat!—   e los cristianos, —¡Santi Yagüe!—" (l. 731) ["The Moors cried out, 'Mahomet!' and the Christians, 'Santiago!'"]. By the time that the combatants seek divine help, thirteen hundred Moors lie smitten on the battlefield, while not a single Spaniard has Death claimed (I^1).

At this point, the narrator takes a well-deserved respite. He summarily professes his admiration in an ecphonesis for the Cid's military prowess and continues, in an asyndeton enumeration, to praise seven men of the Cid's company, which the reader should take as a synecdoche—that is, the praise of individuals constitutes a commendation for the Cid's entire company of valiant horsemen. The passage below, which constitutes a segmental interlude, is ironic in that the narrator has not related any combat activity of any of the mentioned in the passage below:

> ¡Cuál lidia bien   sobre exorado arzón
> mio Cid Ruy Díaz,   el buen lidiador!
> Minaya Álbar Fáñez, que Çorita mandó,
> Martín Antolínez,   el burgalés de pro,
> Muño Gustioz,   que so criado fue,
> Martín Muñoz,   el que mandó a Mont Mayor,
> Álbar Álbarez   e Álbar Salvadórez,
> Galín García,   el bueno de Aragón,
> Félez Muñoz,   so sobrino del Campeador;
> desí adelante,   cuantos que ý son
> acorren la seña e a mio Cid el Canpeador
>   (ll. 733-43)
> [Mounted on his gilded saddle,
> Oh how well fought My Cid, the good warrior!
> And Minaya Álvar Fáñez, who was lord of Zorita;
> Martín Antolínez, worthy man of Burgos;
> Muño Gustioz, whom the Cid had brought up;
> Martín Muñoz, lord of Montemayor;
> Álvar Álvarez and Álvar Salvadórez;
> Galindo García, good man of Aragón;
> Félez Muñoz, nephew of the Battler.
> The whole army then
> went to the aid of the ensign of My Cid the
>   Battler.]

After this calm interlude comes the storm. Now, the narrator zooms in to deal with particular scenes. Abruptly, the narrator informs his reader that the Moors have killed the horse of Minaya Álvar Fáñez and that the latter, together with other companions who have rushed to his side to protect him, continues to do battle with the Moors on foot. The pragmatographia shows him taking out his sword, after he has broken his lance, and valiantly striking his enemies (H[1]). The narrator stylistically constructs his ecphrasis in line 746 by means of the figure alliteration and paroxytone rhyme. He employs the figure alliteration twice. He repeats the sound of the consonant "m" ("metió mano") and, more significantly, he deliberately chooses to highlight his text by iterating the vowel "a" ten times. Of these ten instances, the narrator presents the vowel "a" almost consecutively in the first hemistich. Moreover, since the stressed vowel throughout this line falls mainly on the vowel "a" ("lança" / "á" / "quebrada" / "espada" / "mano"), it is this vowel that regulates the rhythmic movement of the line's sound system. With regard to the narrator's use of interior rhyme, one is assonant-paroxytone ("lança" / "quebrada"), the other, consonant-paroxytone ("quebrada" / "espada").

As splendid as the heroic figure of Minaya Álvar Fáñez appears in this scene, he clearly is in dire need of immediate support. At this point the Cid comes to his nephew's assistance. In what constitutes a segmental interlude, Don Rodrigo, in a grotesque act, kills a Moorish official by slicing him from the waist up and then proceeds to give his nephew the former owner's horse:

> A Minaya Álbar Fáñez   matáronle el cavallo,
> bien lo acorren   mesnadas de cristianos.
> La lança á quebrada,   al espada metió mano;
> maguer de pie,   buenos colpes va dando.
> Violo mio Cid   Ruy Díaz el castellano,
> acostós' a un aguazil   que tenié buen cavallo,
> diol' tal espadada   con el so diestro braço,
> cortól' por la cintura,   el medio echó en campo;
> a Minaya Álbar Fáñez   íval' dar el cavallo:
> —¡Cavalgad, Minaya,   vós sodes el mio diestro braço!
> Oy en este día   de vós abré grand bando;
> firmes son los moros,   aún no's' van del campo.— (ll. 744–55)
>
> [Minaya Álvar Fáñez's horse was killed under him
> and the Christian troops rushed to his aid.
> Though his lance was broken he drew his sword,
> and though scarcely still standing he delivered valiant blows.
> My Cid, Ruy Díaz of Castile, saw this:
> he drew close to a Moorish general riding a fine horse,

>   and with his right arm struck him such a blow with
>   his sword
>   that he severed his body at the waist, throwing half
>   of it to the ground.
>   He gave the horse to Minaya Álvar Fáñez:
>   "Mount, Minaya, you are my right arm!
>   Today I shall want much help from you;
>   the Moors are standing firm and have not fled the
>   field."]

Minaya Álvar Fáñez immediately mounts the steed the Cid has offered him and gallops into the fray with his sword raised: "Cavalgó Minaya, el espada en la mano, / por estas fuerças   fuertemientre lidiando; / a los que alcança   valos delibrando" (ll. 756–58) ["Minaya rode, sword in hand, / cutting his way fiercely through the enemy; / those within his reach he killed"]. He leaves behind a string of thirty-four Moors dead; his elbow streams with Moorish blood:

>   A Minaya Álbar Fáñez   bien l'anda el cavallo,
>   d'aquestos moros   mató treinta e cuatro;
>   espada tajador,   sangriento trae el braço,
>   por el cobdo ayuso la sangre destellando"
>   (ll. 778–81)
>   [Minaya Álvar Fáñez's horse proved a swift
>   animal,
>   and he killed thirty-four of those Moors;
>   his sword cut sharply, and his arm was bloody,
>   the blood flowing down to his elbow."]

Interestingly, in this part of the narrative, the Cid's activity in the battle hardly surfaces. Hence, again, the irony of the above lines 733–43, wherein the narrator went out of his way to applaud the Cid for his valiant conduct in this battle. The section dedicated to the Cid occupies a total of six lines. Inexplicably, the narrator chooses not to develop the scene in which the Cid confronts the Moorish King Fáriz. A summary follows, which contains two cases of interior rhyme: one is assonant-paroxytone ("a"-"e"), the other, consonant-paroxytone ("ado"). The summary relates that the Cid attempts three blows at King Fáriz—trebling is common in folklore literature and one finds numerous instances of it in the Mio Cid epic poem—: two blows fail to connect whereas the third cuts deeply into the king's cuirass, drawing blood from his lorica; it tells of the king's escape; and claims the Cid victorious over the Moorish forces:

> Mio Cid Ruy Díaz,   el que en buen ora nasco,
> al rey Fáriz   tres colpes le avié dado,
> los dos le fallen   e el uno l' ha tomado;
> por la loriga ayuso   la sangre destellando,
> bolvió la rienda   por írsele del campo.
> Por aquél colpe   rancado es el fonsado. (ll. 759–64)
> [My Cid Ruy Díaz, the man born in a favoured hour,
> had delivered three blows at King Fáriz:
> two had missed but one struck him,
> and now blood dripped down his armour.
> He pulled at the reins to flee the battle.
> With that blow the whole army was defeated.]

The last encounter in this second battle deals with Martín Antolínez's simultaneous confrontation with the Moorish King Galve. The ensuing rapid and vivid scene rests on the narrator's use of paratactic structure and of his use of the figures asyndeton and iteratio. The Spaniard's sword strikes his enemy's helmet and loosens the carbuncles on it; then his sword penetrates the helmet and draws blood from the king's head. In an apostrophe to his reader, the narrator adds that King Galve gallops off and escapes:

> Martín Antolínez   un colpe dio a Galve,
> las carbonclas del yelmo   echógelas aparte,
> cortól' el yelmo,   que llegó a la carne;
> sabet, el otro   non ge l'osó esperar.
> Arrancado es   el rey Fáriz e Galve. (ll. 765–69)
> [Martín Antolínez struck Galve a blow
> which shattered the rubies on his helm,
> and cut through it to the flesh.
> I tell you he dared not wait for a second blow.

The kings Fáriz and Galve were defeated.]

The narrator closes this episode with a parenthesis: he informs his reader that King Fáriz takes refuge in Terrer and that King Galve finds shelter in Calatayud (ll. 772–77).[15]

With the enemy vanquished (I^1), the Cid liquidates the initial danger he and his men faced at the hands of their Moorish enemies (K^4), and he returns to the city of Alcocer greatly enriched with the booty acquired from this battle ($\downarrow w^o$), which he generously shares with his army. Subsequently, he comments to Mĭnaya Álvar Fáñez that the lands are too poor to sustain the material needs of his men: "—en esta tierra angosta non podriemos bivir—" (l. 835) ["'in this barren land, we would not survive'"]; he sends his nephew off to visit with King Alfonso with tributes from the victorious battle; and he sells the city to a consortium headed by King Fáriz, for three thousand silver marks (w^o):[16]

Sanó el rey Fáriz,   con él se consejavan;
entre los de Teca   e los de Terrer la casa
e los de Calatayut,   que es más ondrada,
así lo an asmado   e metudo en carta:
vendido les á Alcocer   por tres mill marcos de
                                        plata. (ll. 841–45)
[King Fáriz grew well, and they took counsel with
                                        him.
With the people of Ateca and of the town of
                                        Terrer,
and those of Calatayud, a greater city,
a sum was fixed and an agreement was set down in
                                        writing,
by which My Cid sold them Alcocer for three
                        thousand silver marks.]

The final scene marking the exit of the Cid from Alcocer—where the residents of the city weep and regret his departure—constitutes a segmental interlude. To add pathos to this state of affairs, the narrator employs a parelcon for emphasis, fundamentally repeating, in variant form, the same idea twice: "Cuando mio Cid   el castiello quiso quitar, /

44

moros e moras   tomáronse a quexar" (ll. 851–52) and "Cuando quitó a Alcocer   mio Cid el de Bivar, / moros e moras   compeçaron de llorar" (ll. 855–56). Other stylistic considermations worthy of notice are his use of the figure polyptoton: "moros" / "moras," "Vaste" / "váyante" and that of alliteration, with the stress of the consonant "m" in "moros" / "moras" / "tomáronse," "moros" / "moras" / "compeçaron," and that of the consonant sound "k" in "cuando" / "castiello" / "quiso" / "quitar" / "quexar" and "Cuando" / "quitó" / "Alcocer" / "compeçaron." Finally, the lines below contain the assonant-paroxytone rhymes "a-e" and "a-o": "Vaste" / "delante," "pagados" / "fincamos":

>   Cuando mio Cid   el castiello quiso quitar,
>   moros e moras   tomáronse a quexar:
>   —¡Vaste, mio Cid; nuestras oraciones   váyante
>   delante!
>   Nós pagados fincamos,   señor, de la tu part.—
>   Cuando quitó a Alcocer   mio Cid el de Bivar,
>   moros e moras   compeçaron de llorar. (ll. 851–56)
>   [When My Cid decided to leave the fortress
>   the Moors began to lament, men and women alike.
>   "Are you going, My Cid? Let our prayers go before
>   you!
>   We are very grateful to you, our lord, for what you
>   have done."
>   When My Cid, the man from Vivar, left Alcocer,
>   the Moors began to weep, men and women alike.]

Move 8 (Cantar I)

With the apostrophe to his reader, "Quiérovos dezir   del que en buen ora cinxo espada" (l. 899) ["I want to tell you of the man who girded his sword in a favoured hour"], the narrator, withdrawing the reader from the environs of the court of King Alfonso, resumes his tale of the exiled don Rodrigo. In his apostrophe, the narrator employs the "meanwhile, back at the ranch" diegetic ploy. Move 8 is brief and succinctly reports on various conquests that the Cid makes after he departs from Alcocer. The symbolic transcription of Move 8 follows:

$$aCH^1I^1K^4MN$$

(The above symbolic transcription corresponds to the numerical functions: VIIIa, X, XVI, XVIII, XIX, XXV, and XXVI.)

With an increased number of soldiers in his army, the Cid continues to plunder Moorish territories to survive. In passages that constitute a foreshortening of space and time, the narrator offers his reader a simple enumeration, a synthesis-summarization, of the towns and villages that pay tribute to the Cid: Daroca, Molina, Teruel, and Cella del Canal (ll. 866–69). This brings the Cid in the vicinity of Zaragoza, where he continues to pillage the land in order to keep his coffers filled with monies he uses to pay his soldiers and to purchase provisions for the army (aCH^1I^1). The booty thus acquired by his military raids resolves his and his men's immediate needs (K^4). Minaya Álvar Fáñez returns from visiting with don Alfonso, bringing with him an additional two hundred knights and an extraordinary number of infantrymen. In a segmental interlude, the narrator states that Minaya Álvar Fáñez gives the Cid an account of what transpired between the king and himself and, subsequently, communicates news from family and friends to his fellow comrades-in-arms. This fill-in passage that brings the Cid up to date suggests a parallel structure to the episode in Tale 5 wherein which King Alfonso obtains the latest news regarding the Cid from Minaya Álvar Fáñez (see note 16). Finally, the inhabitants of Zaragoza remedy in part the Cid's difficult task (M), that of having to provide for the needs of his augmented forces, by paying a tribute to don Rodrigo (N). At this point, the Cid finds himself in a territory that, as it so happens, is under the protectorate of the count of Barcelona.

Move 9 (Cantar I)

The Cid's recent incursion within the vicinity of Zaragoza provokes a confrontation with don Ramón Berenguer, count of Barcelona. The symbolic transcription of Move 9 follows:

$$A^{19}BC\uparrow G^2H^1I^1K^4M:\underline{N}:-\{Q\}U-\downarrow:$$
$$N$$

(The above symbolic transcription corresponds to the numerical functions: VIII, IX, X, XI, XV, XVI, XVIII, XIX, XXV, XXVI, {XXVII}, XXX, and XX.)

Don Ramón Berenguer considers don Rodrigo's infringement upon Moorish territories that fall under his political and military sphere of influence as a threat, and he immediately sets out to seek and destroy the armed forces of the Cid. His action amounts to a declaration of war between the two men (A^{19}). The segmental interlude that provides the reader with the etiology of a past insult perpetrated by don Rodrigo against don Ramón—that is, that the Cid had wounded his nephew at the count of Barcelona's court (ll. 961-63)—which explains why the count is so ill-disposed already toward the Battler, is an unnecessary anamnesis. The dispensable retrospection brings with it, in turn, a needless narrative component to the epic poem in that it reveals a deliberate attempt on the narrator's part to control and dictate his reader's response to the count of Barcelona by means of a negative illocutionary appraisal of don Ramón's character: "El conde es muy follón   e dixo una vanidat" (l. 960) ["The Count was boastful and spoke vain words"]. The anamnesis is superfluous because it has no bearing on the present state of alienation that don Ramón harbors against don Rodrigo. The Cid's actions, from the vantage point of the Frank, demonstrates a total disregard of and disrespect for don Ramón's political authority and, thereby constitute an insult against his person: "llegaron las nuevas   al conde de Barcilona / que mio Cid Ruy Díaz   que l' corrié la tierra toda; / ovo grand pesar   e tóvos'lo a grand fonta (ll. 957-59) ["A report came to the ears of the Count of Barcelona / that My Cid Ruy Díaz was ravaging all his lands; / he was greatly troubled and considered himself offended"].

The passages regarding the count's journey to Tévar to confront the Cid: "tres días e dos noches   pensaron de andar, / alcançaron a mio Cid   en Tévar e el pinar" (ll. 970-71) ["They rode for three days and two nights / and they reached My Cid in the pine wood at Tévar"]) and that of the Cid's march to Tévar: "Mio Cid don Rodrigo   ganancia trae grand, / dice de una sierra   e llegava a un val" (ll. 973-74) ["My Cid Don Rodrigo carried great booty with him; / he rode down from a hill into a valley"]), reveal that, besides being synchronic, both actions constitute examples of spatial and temporal foreshortening. The following passage contains stylistic features of interest that serve to underscore the semantic content of the passage. There is the use of the figure iteratio: "grand" / "grand"; that of the polyptoton: "grand" / "Grandes," "tuertos" / "tuerto," and "llegándose" / "allegan"); that of the uncommon epanalepsis: "Grandes son los poderes e apriessa llegándose van, / entre moros e cristianos gentes se le allegan grandes" (ll. 967–68), and the epanalepsis variant: "—Grandes tuertos me tiene mio Cid el de Bivar, / dentro en mi cort tuerto me tovo grand—" (ll. 961–62); and that of the equally rare (variant of) antimetabole: "Grandes tuertos me tiene" / "tuerto me tovo grand." With regard to prosody, this passage contains several assonant as well as consonant interior rhymes. Among the first, there is one case of an acute (oxytone) rhyme "a" in a single line: "ovo grand pesar e tóvos'lo a grand fonta" (l. 959), and there are numerous cases of paroxytone rhymes—for example, "e-o": "tuertos" / "dentro" / "tuerto," "e-e": "poderes"/ "gentes," "a-o": "alcançaron" / "esforçado" / "manos," and "e-a": "nuevas" / "tierra" and "apriessa" / "allegan." Among the second—that is, consonant rhymes—there is the paroxytone rhyme "ovo": "ovo" / "tóvo"; "aron": "pensaron" / "alcançaron"; and that of "andes": "Grandes" / "grandes." Finally, of interest is the narrator's criticism of the count of Barcelona in line 960: "—El conde es muy follón—," in that he switches from the use of indefinite preterite to the present tense of the indicative mood, a tense generally employed by omniscient narrators to comment on their diegesis:

> Llegaron las nuevas al conde de Barcilona
> que mio Cid Ruy Díaz que l' corrié la tierra toda;
> ovo grand pesar e tóvos'lo a grand fonta.
> El conde es muy follón e dixo una vanidat:
> —Grandes tuertos me tiene mio Cid el de Bivar,
> dentro en mi cort tuerto me tovo grand,
> firióm' el sobrino e no'n' lo enmendó más;
> agora córrem' las tierras que en mi enpara están.
> Non lo desafié ni l' torné amistad,
> mas, cuando él me lo busca, írgelo he yo
>   demandar.—
> Grandes son los poderes e apriessa llegándose
>   van,
> entre moros e cristianos gentes se le allegan
>   grandes.
> Adeliñan tras mio Cid, el bueno de Bivar,

> tres días e dos noches   pensaron de andar,
> alcançaron a mio Cid   en Tévar e el pinar;
> así viene esforçado el conde   que a manos se le cuidó tomar. (ll. 957–72)

[A report came to the ears of the Count of Barcelona
that My Cid Ruy Díaz was ravaging all his lands;
He was greatly troubled and considered himself offended.
The Count was [*sic*] boastful and spoke vain words:
"My Cid, the man from Vivar, has greatly wronged me!
In my court he wronged me greatly.
He wounded my nephew and has done nothing to make amends,
and now he is ravaging lands under my protection.
I have never challenged him or ceased to be friendly towards him,
but since he seeks trouble with me I must go and demand redress."
His forces were great and assembled rapidly;
he gathered together many men, both Moors and Christians.
They went in search of My Cid, good man of Vivar.
They rode for three days and two nights
and they reached My Cid in the pine wood at Tévar.
The Count came with so great a force that he expected to take the Cid prisoner.]

Notified that the count of Barcelona does not wish him well, the Cid endeavors to assuage the charges leveled against him by the count of Barcelona (B): "—Digades al conde   non lo tengo a mal, / de lo so non lievo nada,   déxem' ir en paz—" (ll. 977–78) ["'Tell the Count not to take things badly; / I am taking nothing of his, / and he should allow me to go in peace'"]. Attempts at reconciliation fail, and don Rodrigo realizes that his sole choice is to engage the count of Barcelona in battle: "Tornós' el mandadero   cuanto pudo más; / essora lo coñosce   mio Cid el de Bivar / que a menos de batalla   no s' pueden den quitar" (ll. 982–84)

["The messenger returned as fast as he could. / Now My Cid, the man from Vivar, realized / that there was no other way but to fight"]. In the following passage—one that contains several assonant rhymes: that of the paroxytone rhyme "e-o" ("cavalleros" / metedos"), that of "a-a" ("sobejanas" / "batalla" / "nada"), that of "a-o"("darnos" / "cristianos"), and that of the rhyme of the assonant acute "a" in line 990 ("adelant" / irán")—the Cid decides to confront militarily don Ramón and instructs his men to prepare themselves for the imminent clash that will shortly ensue (C):

    —¡Ya cavalleros,   apart fazed la ganancia,
    apriessa vos guarnid   e metedos en las armas!
    El conde don Remont   darnos ha grant batalla,
    de moros e de cristianos   gentes trae sobejanas,
    a menos de batalla   non nos dexarié por nada.
    Pues adelant irán tras nós,   aquí sea la batalla;
    apretad los cavallos   e bistades las armas.—
                                        (ll. 985–91)
["Now, my knights, put the booty to one side.
Be quick to equip and arm yourselves;
Count Don Ramón is to engage us in a great battle;
he has a vast army of Moors and Christians,
and he would not leave us in peace without a
                                          battle.
Since they will pursue us wherever we go, let the
                                        battle be fought here.
Tighten the saddle-girths and arm yourselves."]

    The Cid and his men attack (↑). The battle between the two armies takes place in an open field (H^1). The battle scene constitutes an instance of temporal foreshortening in that it transpires in less than three lines: "los pendones e las lanças   tan bien las van enpleando, / a los unos firiendo   e a los otros derrocando. / Vencido á esta batalla   el que en buen ora nasco" (ll. 1006–8) ["The lances with their pennants were used to great effect, / striking some and unseating others. / The man born in a favoured hour won the battle"]. Victorious (I^1), don Rodrigo takes the count prisoner and thus liquidates any military threat to his faction (K^4). In passing, the Cid obtains significant booty from this brief skirmish with the

Franks, including the count's famous sword, Colada. At this juncture, don Rodrigo proposes a difficult task to don Ramón (M), namely, that he break bread with him at his table. The count of Barcelona refuses to touch a morsel of the food placed before him. The narrator underscores his denial by using the figure diazeugma, sentences where multiple verbs have a single subject (N -): "—Non combré un bocado   por cuanto ha en toda España, / antes perderé el cuerpo   e dexaré el alma—" (ll. 1021–22) ["'I will not eat a mouthful, for all the wealth in Spain; / I would rather die and give up my soul'"]. Don Ramón persists in this attitude even when the Cid promises to give him his freedom, a promise to which he attaches a harsh cataplexis. In his cataplexis, which contains an isocolon, the Cid threatens to punish the count of Barcelona severely if he does not dine: "—Comed, conde, d'este pan   e beved d'este vino; / si lo que digo fiziéredes   saldredes de cativo, / si non, en todos vuestros días   non veredes cristianismo—" (ll. 1025–27) ["'Come, Count, eat this bread and drink this wine. / If you do what I say you will be set free; / if not, in all your days you will never again see Christian lands'"]. To both the Cid's promise and his menace, don Ramón remains steadfast, indifferent, adamantly rejecting once again the Cid's overture (N-): "Dixo el conde: —Comede, don Rodrigo e pensedes de folgar, / que yo dexarm'é morir,   que non quiero yantar—" (ll. 1028–29) ["Count Don Ramón said: 'You eat, Don Rodrigo, and take your rest, / for I shall let myself die; I will not eat'"].

Three days later, the situation changes. The reference to the passage of three days appears in a single line and, thus, constitutes another temporal foreshortening. The Cid now adopts a different tactic. He gives don Ramón his word that he will set him and his two captive men free if he eats to the Cid's satisfaction: "—e si vós comiéredes   don yo sea pagado, / a vós   e a dos fijosdalgo / quitarvos he los cuerpos   e darvos é de mano—" (ll. 1034–35b) ["'but if you eat enough to please me, / both you and two of your noblemen / will be set free and sent on your way'"]. With this assurance, don Ramón acquiesces to the Cid's request and sits down at the table, eating to his heart's content (N): "Con los cavalleros que el Cid le avié dados, / comiendo va el conde,   ¡Dios, qué de buen grado!" (ll. 1051–52) ["With the knights that the Cid had brought to him, / the Count began to eat—Lord God with what pleasure!"]. By so complying, the count of Barcelona tacitly recognizes his foe as a hero {Q}.

Having fulfilled the difficult task, don Ramón and his captive soldiers depart from the Cid's camp as free, albeit humiliated, men (U-↓). Triumphant, don Rodrigo leaves Tévar, as well (↓).[17]

>*Move 10 (Cantar II)*
>This move is brief. Its symbolic transcription follows:

$$a^5C\uparrow\{H^1I^1\}K^4$$

(The above symbolic transcription corresponds to the numerical functions: VIIIa, X, XI, {XVI, XVIII}, and XIX.)

Cantar II begins with the narrator disclosing that the Cid abandons the three geographic locations of Zaragoza, Huesa, and Montalbán and heads eastward toward the "mar salada" (l. 1090) ["salt sea"] (C↑). Financially, don Rodrigo's needs do not abide (a^5). Indeed, the Cid explicitly refuses to return to the count of Barcelona any of the booty don Ramón had forfeited to him:

>—Sabet, non vos daré   a vós un dinero malo,
>ca huebos me lo he   e pora estos mios vassallos
>que conmigo   andan lazrados.
>Prendiendo de vós e de otros   irnos hemos
>   pagando.—" (l. 1042, ll. 1044–46)
>["I tell you I shall not give you a rotten pennyworth;
>no, all that you have lost I shall not give back,
>for I need it for these my vassals,
>who suffer hardship with me; I shall not give it back!
>We shall satisfy ourselves by taking from you and
>   others"].

As for the Cid's new conquests, the narrator summarily informs the reader in a spatial and temporal foreshortening passage that don Rodrigo, without much ado, takes Jérica, Onda, Almenar, Burriana, and Murviedro (ll. 1092–95), thus rendering tacit all battle engagements and victories over the Moors ($\{H^1I^1\}$). The conquests bring with them booty and don Rodrigo, once again, momentarily liquidates the persisting need to refill his coffers with money (K^4).

Move 11 (Cantar II)

The following is a symbolic transcription of the Cid's victory over an unexpected preemptive attack by an anonymous, unidentified contingent from Valencia:

$$A^{19}B^4C\uparrow H^1I^1K^4\downarrow MN$$

(The above symbolic transcription corresponds to the numerical functions: VIII, IX, X, XI, XVI, XVIII, XIX, XX, XXV, and XXVI.)

Faced with the recent victories of the Cid, the Moors of Valencia decide to launch a preemptive offensive against the Cid (A^{19}) and set up their camp at the outskirts of Murviedro, a city occupied by the Cid and his army. Informed of the presence of enemy cavalry and troops, the Cid welcomes the opportunity to test his might against them. Note, however, the Cid's humanity as he first recognizes the right of these people to be hostile toward the Spaniards since it is the Spaniards who are here the aggressors and the spoilers of the land: "—En sus tierras somos e fémosles todo mal, / bevemos so vino e comemos el so pan; / si nos cercar vienen, con derecho lo fazen—" (ll. 1103–5) ["'We are in their lands and are doing them all possible wrong, / we are drinking their wine and eating their bread; / if they come and besiege us, they have every right to do so'"]. To confront the new situation, the Cid sends out requests to his forces stationed in Jérica, Olocau, Onda, Almenar, and Burriana to assist him in this new venture (B^4). Three days later these forces arrive and join those of the Cid. Deliberating as to how to deal with this new problem, don Rodrigo accepts the following strategy proposed by Minaya Álvar Fáñez: Minaya Álvar Fáñez will charge one flank with a hundred horsemen while the Cid, with the remaining cavalry, will charge another, thus attacking the Moors in a pincer-type movement (C):

—A mí dedes ciento cavalleros, que non vos pido más,
vós con los otros firádeslos delant,
bien los ferredes, que dubda non ý avrá;
yo con los ciento entraré del otra part,
commo fío por Dios, el campo nuestro será.—
(ll. 1129–33)

["Give me one hundred knights, I ask no more of you; you with the others attack them from the front, striking resolutely and without fear; I with the hundred will attack from behind. As I trust in God, the field of battle will be ours."]

The forces of the Cid leave the confines of the city ($\uparrow$) at dawn on the fourth day and initiate their attack against the Moors in an open field (H^1). The narrator renders the central core of the combat in an unusual manner. The Cid issues his order to charge the enemy: "—¡En el nombre del Criador   e del apóstol Santi Yagüe, / feridlos, cavalleros,   d'amor e de grand voluntad, / ca yo só Ruy Díaz,   mio Cid el de Bivar!—" (ll. 1138–40) ["'In the name of the Creator and Saint James the Apostle, / strike them, my knights, with all your heart and strength and will, / for I am Ruy Díaz, My Cid of Vivar!'"]. But as soon as the Cid commands the charge, the Spaniards, in another passage that evinces a foreshortening of space and time, vanquish the Moors. The narrative is as brief as it is vivid. The narrator frames his compressed pragmatographia in an apostrophe to his reader in which he invites, even forces, the reader to imagine the action. He accomplishes this by means of a metonymic enumeration wherein he substitutes effect for cause. Hence, it is the reader who, consequently, must provide the agency lacking in this battle. In short, the narrator forces his reader to respond to his text as a co-creator. The reader must create in his mind's eye not only the agents responsible for the resultant state of affairs, but also the activity of said agents: "Tanta cuerda de tienda   ý veriedes quebrar, / arrancarse las estacas   e acostarse los tendales" (ll. 1141–42) ["You could see so many ropes cut, / stakes pulled up and on all sides tent poles thrown to the ground"].

The Cid's soldiers kill two Moorish kings, an occurrence that the narrator reports in an illocutionary declarative statement in a matter-of-fact manner: "Dos reyes de moros   mataron en es alcaz" (l. 1147) ["They killed two Moorish kings in that pursuit"]. Then the Cid drives the Moors back to Valencia (I^1). The victory eliminates the initial threat that don Rodrigo faced from his enemy (K^4), and he and his men return with their unspecified booty to Murviedro ($\downarrow$).[18] Subsequently, don Rodrigo and his army undertake the difficult task of conquering a series of towns in the surrounding areas—actions that involve spatial and temporal foreshortening—tasks that they easily accomplish (M N). Move 11 terminates with the narrator informing the reader—in a passage that, once more, constitutes a spatial and temporal foreshortening—that the Cid and his men spend the next three years engaged in such labors: "En tierra de moros, prendiendo e ganando, / e durmiendo los días e las noches trasnochando, / en ganar aquellas villas mio Cid duró tres años" (ll. 1167–69) ["In the domain of the Moors, taking and conquering, / sleeping by day and marching by night, / My Cid spent three years overcoming those towns"].

Move 12 (Cantar II)
Move 12 deals with the Cid's conquest of Valencia. The symbolic transcription of this action follows:

$$aB^4C\uparrow G^2H^1\text{-}I^1var.K^4$$

(The above symbolic transcription corresponds to the numerical functions: VIIIa, IX, X, XI, XV, XVI, XVIII, and XIX.)

Don Rodrigo's previous victories underscore the Cid's need to conquer Valencia in order to establish his dominion over this geographical region (a). This fact has not escaped the attention of the residents of this urban center, as evidenced by their failed effort to draw the king of Morocco into the fray on their behalf. To undertake this major military operation, the Cid seeks the assistance of his compatriots in Navarre, Aragón, and Castile (B^4). With an augmented number of soldiers at his disposal, the Cid and his army depart from Murviedro and travel on horseback (and on foot) to Valencia ($C\uparrow G^2$). Upon his arrival at Valencia, don Rodrigo immediately blockades the city, which leads to the city's fall after only nine months. The surrender of the residents of Valencia constitutes a variant of function XVI—The Hero and the Villain Join in Direct Combat—and function XVIII—The Villain Is Defeated in open combat—(H^1-I^1var.): "Nueve meses complidos, sabet, sobr'ella yaz, / cuando vino el dezeno oviérongela a dar" (ll. 1209–10) ["[H]e waited there for a full nine months, I tell you, / and when the tenth month came the city surrendered"]. Clearly, the fall of Valencia to don Rodrigo liquidates the lack mentioned above (K^4).

Move 13 (Cantar II)
Move 13 deals with the Cid's victory over the king of Seville, who counterattacks to liberate Valencia from don Rodrigo's control. The symbolic transcription of this move follows:

$$A^{19}C\uparrow H^1 I^1 K^4 \downarrow w^o$$

(The above symbolic transcription corresponds to the numerical functions: VIII, X, XI, XVI, XVIII, XIX, XX, and XXXI.)

Upon hearing of the Cid's conquest of Valencia, the king of Seville declares war on the Cid (A^{19}). In what amounts to still another spatial and temporal foreshortening, the king leaves Seville in one line; in the next line he and his army of thirty thousand men (note the narrator's fondness for the figure hyperbole) are found at the outskirts of Valencia. Immediately upon his arrival, the king of Seville engages the Cid in battle in an open field ($C\uparrow H^1$). The introductory five-line passage is rich in interior rhyme. There is the assonant and consonant paroxytone rhyme "a-a" and "ava," respectively: "folgava" / "campañas" / "llegava"; the assonant-paroxytone rhyme "e-a": "presa" / "Valencia" / "treinta" / "huerta"; and the assonant-oxytone rhyme of the "e": "aquél" / "rey" and "ver" / "aprés." Note, also, the narrator's conscious and careful use of the figure alliteration—namely, that of the accented vowel "e" consecutively repeated four times—to report to the Cid the fall of Valencia ("que presa es Valencia"):

> Ya folgava mio Cid   con todas sus conpañas;
> a aquel rey de Sevilla   el mandado llegava
> que presa es Valencia,   que no ge la enparan.
> Vínolos ver   con treinta mill de armas,
> aprés de la huerta   ovieron la batalla. (ll. 1221–25)
> [Now, while My Cid was resting with his troops,
> word reached the renowned King of Seville
> that Valencia had been taken as it could no longer be defended;
> he came to fight My Cid's men with thirty thousand warriors.
> Near to the plantations the battle was fought.]

In this rather undefined battle, the Moorish soldiers appear to drown. This impression is conveyed by the figure circumlocution: "En el passar de Xúcar ý veriedes barata, / moros en aruenço amidos bever agua" (ll. 1228–29) ["At the crossing of the Júcar you could see great confusion — / the Moors struggling against the current and drinking the water against their will"]. Next, the narrator tells rather than shows his reader in an illocutionary declarative statement that the king of Seville escaped after receiving three wounds: "Aquel rey de Sevilla con tres colpes escapa" (l. 1230) {"<That> [t]hat king of Seville escapes after <receiving, suffering> three blows"}. The victory of the Cid over the Moors (I^1) liquidates the threat that the king of Seville had posed to don Rodrigo. Lastly, the Cid returns to Valencia with the booty won in this battle ($K^4 \downarrow w^o$).[19, 20]

Move 14 (Cantar II)

Move 14 concerns the reunification of the Cid's family in Valencia. Below is the symbolic transcription of this move.

$$aBC\uparrow\{G^2\}L\text{-}MN\downarrow Qw^2$$

(The above symbolic transcription corresponds to the numerical functions: VIIIa, IX, X, XI, {XV}, XXIV, XXV, XXVI, XX, XXVII, and XXXI.)

The Cid, now the undisputed lord of Valencia, is still without his family (a). To resolve this lack, he sends Minaya Álvar Fáñez with gifts to King Alfonso, instructing his nephew to request, on his behalf, that the king allow his wife and his daughters to join him in Valencia (B). Minaya Álvar Fáñez accepts this contract (C); leaves Valencia ($\uparrow$); visits with Alfonso in Carrión—spatial transference from one kingdom to another on horseback is tacit $\{G^2\}$; gives the king the gifts the Cid has sent; and pleads don Rodrigo's case (L-)—that is, he requests that the king allow the Cid's wife and daughters to join him in Valencia. This petition creates a difficult task for King Alfonso (M), who up to this point has accepted gifts of tribute from the Cid, but has neither considered it appropriate to pardon his former vassal nor to allow the family of the Cid to join him in exile. The king consents to don Rodrigo's request and his assent marks the resolution of the difficult task (N). Minaya Álvar Fáñez departs for the monastery of Saint Peter of Cardeña and, after a brief encounter with

Raquel and Vidas, the two Jewish businessmen who came to the economic assistance of don Rodrigo at the start of the *Cantar de Mio Cid*, departs for Valencia together with doña Jimena and her two daughters, doña Elvira and doña Sol ($\downarrow$).[21] In Valencia the Cid celebrates the arrival of his wife and of his two daughters (Q) and resumes not only his domestic marital relationship with doña Jimena, but also his domestic role as a parent (w^2). Segmental interludes are created through the conversations that Minaya Álvar Fáñez holds with Raquel and Vidas, with the Cid's family at the monastery of Saint Peter of Cardeña, and with Abengalbón, a Moorish friend of the Cid, in Molina, along with the conversation that the Cid engages with his men, whom he sends out to meet the approaching retinue of Minaya Álvar Fáñez[22, 23]

Move 15 (Cantar III)
Move 15 deals with don Rodrigo vanquishing King Yúsuf of Morocco at Valencia. The symbolic transcription follows:

$$A^{19}C\uparrow:H:^1I:^1K^4\downarrow w°W*var.$$

(The above symbolic transcription corresponds to the numerical functions: VIII, X, XI, XVI, XVIII, XIX, XX, and XXXI [2].)

Move 15 serves two purposes. On the one hand, it is ornamental in nature. From this point of reference, the reader of the *Cantar de Mio Cid* can view the King Yúsuf incident as an extensive segmental interlude, since it allows the self-conscious Cid to showcase himself as a hero before his wife, daughters, and their ladies-in-waiting. Indeed, the Cid is the first to admit this intention as he joyously states in the following assonant-paroxytone rhyme "i-o": "—Venido m'es delicio   de tierras d'allent mar—" (l. 1639) ["Good fortune has come to me from beyond the sea"]. More importantly, however, is don Rodrigo's subsequent use of a parelcon: "—verán por los ojos—" (l. 1643) ["'With their own eyes they shall see'"]. His words emphasize that life in exile, in lands hostile to Christians, is fraught with hardship and danger:

    —¡Grado al Criador   e a Santa María madre,
    mis fijas e mi mugier,   que las tengo acá!
    Venido m'es delicio   de tierras d'allent mar,
    entraré en las armas,   non lo podré dexar;

       mis fijas e mi mugier   verme an lidiar,
       en estas tierras agenas   verán las moradas cómmo
                                                se fazen,
       afarto verán por los ojos   cómmo se gana el pan.—
       Su mugier e sus fijas subiólas al alcácer.
                                                (ll. 1637–44)
["Thanks be to the Creator and to Saint Mary the
                                              Holy Mother
that I have my daughters and my wife here with me!
Good fortune has come to me from beyond the sea;
I shall take up arms, it must be so.
My daughters and my wife will see me fight.
They will see what life is like in these alien lands.
With their own eyes they shall see full well how we
                                              earn our bread."
He took his wife and daughters up to the citadel.]

    On the other hand, the encounter with the Moorish forces of King Yúsuf is of capital structural importance on several counts. First, his victory over King Yúsuf allows don Rodrigo to affirm his reign in the region against the Moors, and it elevates him to the level of a sovereign in that he commits an act pertaining to the domain of a monarch. At this point in the narrative, the Cid is beholden to no one: he is a self-made man. But ironically, even paradoxically, he is beholden to King Alfonso, since it was the king who forced don Rodrigo into exile, which eventually led to the Cid's subsequent conquest of Valencia. The Cid's victory over the Moors gives rise subsequently to the termination of don Rodrigo's long-endured political exile from the court of King Alfonso and to King Alfonso's decree that the Cid's two daughters, doña Elvira and doña Sol, wed don Fernando and don Diego, the infantes of Carrión.

    Evidently free from his previous military commitment, King Yúsuf, irate over the military conquests of don Rodrigo, decides to regain Valencia. In what amounts to both a telescoping of space and a foreshortening of time, King Yúsuf crosses the Mediterranean Sea and has his army of fifty thousand men pitch their tents at the outskirts of Valencia's city limits. This hostile act constitutes a declaration of war against the Cid (A^{19}). Don Rodrigo is joyous over this last Moorish event for, as indicated in the passage cited above, it will enable him to engage in battle with his family demostrating how he must existentially earn his keep. With an army of nearly four thousand men, the Cid prepares to arm himself. Here the reader finds an antithesis that serves to create tension. That is, while the Cid rejoices overtly over the present state of affairs—his ecphonetic paeanismus constitutes an outcry of joy: "Alegrávas' mio Cid e dixo: —¡Tan buen día es oy!—" (l. 1659) ["My Cid spoke joyfully: 'What a day this is!'"]—the women, in contrast, recoil, steadfastly gripped with terror: "Miedo á su mugier e quiérel' quebrar el coraçón, / assí fazié a las dueñas e a sus fijas amas a dos, / del día que nasquieran non vieran tal tremor" (ll. 1660–62) ["His wife was so terrified it seemed her heart would burst, / and so too were her ladies and her two daughters. / Since the day of their birth they had never heard such a thunderous noise"]. However, the women soon lose thir fear after don Rodrigo assures them that all will end well: "Alegres son las dueñas, perdiendo van el pavor" (l. 1670) ["The ladies, in their joy, gradually lost their fear"].

With the sound and fury of enemy drums shattering the air and Moorish horsemen intrepidly galloping through the fields, the plantations of Valencia, the Cid and his cavalry leave the city to engage the army of King Yúsuf in a battle in an open field (C↑H^1). Interestingly and ironically, the narrator, after the previous buildup, does not trouble to offer his reader a pragmatographia of the battle itself. Instead, he presents the situation in an illoculationary speech in which he summarizes facts. In the first day of this two-day military engagement with the Moors, the Cid's cavalry charges bravely. The Spaniards drive the Moorish cavalry out of the plantations and back to their camp and they slay five hundred of King Yúsuf's men. The narrator's paratactic rendition is cut and dry: "do's' fallan con los moros cometiénlos tan aína, / sácanlos de las huertas mucho a fea guisa, / quinientos mataron d'ellos conplidos en es día" (ll. 1676–78) ["When they encountered the Moors, they were quick to attack. / In brutal conflict they drove them out of the plantations, / killing a full hundred of them that day"]. The lines in which the Cid compliments his men for a job well done that day (lines 1685-90*b*) and his final and brief, but to the point, exhortation to his men (line 1691), constitute segmental interludes. With regard to the Cid's exhortation, his use of the figures metonymy and a variant protrope connote an implicit threat as to what awaits them if they fail to defeat the Moors as well as a tacit promise of continuous prosperity if they do: "—¡Más vale que nós los vezcamos que ellos cojan el pan!—" (l. 1691) ["'It is better that we defeat them than allow them to take our food!'"].

Next, there occurs a temporal foreshortening: day passes into night and night gives way to predawn hours. After hearing mass, the Cid's forces of just under four thousand "a los cincuaenta mill vanlos ferir de grado" (l. 1718) ["went forth eagerly to strike the fifty thousand"]. (Surprisingly, the narrator has forgotten that the Spaniards had vanquished five hundred Moors the day before.) The diegesis of the battle is, once again, brief; details are sparse. Minaya Álvar Fáñez attacks with one hundred and thirty horsemen. (Note that his petition to the Cid to put a determined number of the cavalry under his command is a leitmotif associated with Minaya Álvar Fáñez). The Cid, as well, attacks with the remaining men. The narrator renders the Cid's action in this battle through the use of the figures hyperbole, alliteration (of the consonant "m"), scesis onomaton (line 1724 lacks a conjugated verb), and an interior rhyme stressing an acute "o" ("enpleó" / "metió"): "Mio Cid enpleó la lança, al espada metió mano, / atantos mata de moros que non fueron contados, / por el cobdo ayuso la sangre destellando" (ll. 1722–24) ["My Cid wielded his lance and then drew his sword; / he killed Moors beyond reckoning, / as their blood flowed down to his elbow"]. King Yúsuf avoids three blows (another case of trebling) from the Cid's sword and manages to escape, finding refuge within a castle in Cullera. All told, the Cid's forces thrash the Moors and, within a context of an extravagant hyperbole, kill nearly fifty thousand Moors in two days (I^1): "Los cincuaenta mill por cuenta fueron notados, / non escaparon más de ciento e cuatro" (ll. 1734–35) ["The fifty thousand Moors were accounted for; / only one hundred and four had escaped"]. In passing, the narrator registers neither any wounded nor dead among the Cid's army of just under four thousand. With this victory the Cid has liquidated the threat posed by King Yúsuf at the outset of this move (K^4).[24]

At this point, the Cid returns to Valencia ($\downarrow$), where he places at the feet of the ladies his booty (w^0), which includes three thousand marks in silver and gold plus other items. His wife, daughters, and their entourage, who witnessed the battle from the Cid's castle in Valencia, recognize the Cid as a hero (Q). Subsequently, don Rodrigo commits an extraordinary act: he dares to assume the role of a king, taking it upon himself to marry the women in doña Jimena's service to men under his command. Most interestingly, he is exceedingly eager that those in Castile receive news of his unprecedented and provocative act (W*var.):

> —Estas dueñas que aduxiestes,   que vos sirven tanto,
> quiérolas casar   con de aquestos mios vassallos;
> a cada una d'ellas   doles dozientos marcos,
> que lo sepan en Castiella   a quién sirvieron tanto.— (ll. 1764–67)
> ["These ladies you brought with you, who give such loyal service,
> I wish to marry to some of my vassals.
> I give to each one of them two hundred silver marks,
> that it may be known in Castile to whom they have given such loyal service."]

This last event is important in still another way in that it highlights the fact that the Cid has married all the women in his immediate circle with the exception of his daughters, doña Elvira and doña Sol. From a structural point of view, it is clear that if the narrator is to bring closure to his work, he must first marry off the two daughters of don Rodrigo.

Finally, with the regal actions described above, the Cid has become a de facto king in his own right, beholden to no one. Don Rodrigo's geographical displacement is one of being in a state of exile without return. Henceforth, indeed, the Cid will never emotionally yearn to return to Vivar again. Don Rodrigo's physical exile from Vivar terminates with his having led his men to a new and promised land. The Cid and his entourage, in effect, have adopted a new homeland. From this day forward, his residence in Valencia is permanent. With this literary mythopoetic variant of the archetypal mythopoetic tale of Exodus as well as that of The Book of Joshua in the Hebrew Bible, the geographical exile of the Cid draws to a close.[25]

Move 16 (Cantar III)

Move 16 deals with don Rodrigo obtaining full pardon from King Alfonso and of his becoming, once again, a vassal of King Alfonso. The symbolic transcription of this move follows:

$$aBC\uparrow G^2L\text{-}MNQw^o$$

(The above symbolic transcription corresponds to the numerical functions: VIIIa, IX, X, XI, XV, XXIV, XXV, XXVI, XXVII, and XXXI.) In spite of his material triumphs and the multiple gifts he has bestowed on King Alfonso, the Cid continues to be a political exile from the court of King Alfonso (a). This predicament, however, is soon to change. Minaya Álvar Fañez and Martín Antolínez, who have returned from visiting with King Alfonso, inform the Cid (B) of the king's wish:

> Esto diziendo, conpieçan la razón,
> lo que'l' rogava Alfonso el de León
> de dar sus fijas a los ifantes de Carrión,
> que'l' coñoscié ý ondra e creçrié en onor,
> que ge lo consejava d'alma e de coraçón."
> (ll. 1926–30)
> [When he had said this, they began to put to him
> the request made by Alfonso of León
> that he give his daughters in marriage to the Infantes
> of Carrión.
> The King, seeing that My Cid would gain honour and
> greater wealth,
> with both heart and soul advised him to consent."]

Segmental interludes are created by the conversation that ensues among don Rodrigo, Minaya Álvar Fañez, and Martín Antolínez regarding this issue, plus the exchange of letters between the Cid and the king to establish the time and geographical location where their interview is to take place to discuss the marriage of doña Elvira and that of doña Sol to don Fernando and don Diego. Three weeks later don Rodrigo, who must obey the command of King Alfonso, leaves for the banks of the Tajo River to meet with the king and his retinue ($C\uparrow G^2$). The king, informed of the Cid's proximity to his camp, departs with a small entourage to greet him. Facing King Alfonso, don Rodrigo kneels humbly before his monarch and, amid the king's retinue and his own men, in a heartfelt ecphonetic optatio, requests that the king grant him full pardon (L-): "—¡Merced vos pido a vós, mio natural señor! / Assí estando, dédesme vuestra amor, / que lo oyan cuantos aquí son—" (ll. 2031-32b) ["'I beg a favour of you, as my natural lord! / As I kneel before you, I ask that you grant me your love; / may all those present be my witnesses'"]. King Alfonso immediately resolves the difficult task (M) assigned to him by the Cid by granting don Rodrigo his pardon (N) and by receiving his hero (Q) back into the fold as his vassal—an act on the king's part that constitutes a reward for the Cid's past comportment toward his person (w^o). Stylistically, the intensity of the king's expression of appreciation and love for the Cid results from his use of the figures isocolon ("d'alma" / "de coraçón"), diazeugma ("feré" / "perdono" / "dovos"), and prozeugma (of the conjugated verb "feré"): "Dixo el rey:—Esto feré d'alma e de coraçón. / Aquí vos perdono e dovos mi amor / e en todo mio reino parte desde oy—" (ll. 2033-35) ["The King replied: 'This I will do with my heart and soul! / Here and now I pardon you and grant you my love, / and from today I give you a place in my kingdom'"].

The resolution of the Cid's political stand with respect to King Alfonso brings closure to Tale 1. The Tale of the Exile of Rodrigo Díaz, the Cid.

Chapter 4. The Tale of Fernando González and Diego González, the Infantes of Carrión

The eleventh tale of the *Cantar de Mio Cid* tells of the marriages of Fernando González and Diego González, the infantes of Carrión, to Elvira Díaz and Sol Díaz, the daughters of doña Jimena and the Cid. This tale, as well, describes the subsequent termination of these unions. The diegesis of don Fernando and don Diego consists of eight moves.

Move 1 (Cantar II)
Move 1 encompasses the lay contract leading to the marriages of the infantes of Carrión to the daughters of the Cid. The symbolic transcription of this move is given below:

$$\alpha\gamma^2\delta a^{1,5} BC\uparrow\{G^2\}DE\S\uparrow:G:^2MNw^1\downarrow$$

(The above symbolic transcription corresponds to the numerical functions: II, III, VIIIa, IX, X, XI, {XV}, XII, XIII, XI, XV, XXV, XXVI, and XXXI.)

The initial situation (α) includes three events. The first occurrence relates to the Cid's taking of Valencia. The second episode deals with don Rodrigo's victory over the (anonymous) Moorish king of Seville, who attempts to retake Valencia with his army. The third incident refers to Minaya Álvar Fáñez's trip to Carrión to deliver to King Alfonso a wealth of gifts from the Cid. Present when the Cid's tribute passes into the hands of the king are the infantes of Carrión, though at this stage of the diegesis they are not yet named. At the sight of the immense wealth the Cid has managed to amass, the infantes, out of base greed, begin to take an interest in doña Elvira and doña Sol, the daughters of the Cid. At this point, however, they are reluctant to form a formal alliance with the Cid through the institution of marriage. They are exceedingly conscious that they descend from a family of ancient, noble, and famous lineage, whereas the Cid's social credentials place him within the lower echelons of those of aristocratic rank. Hence, marriage to the daughters of the Cid does not constitute, at least for the moment, a normal, viable social state of affairs for them. Conversing among themselves—interestingly, the narrator renders the dialogue between don Fernando and don Diego not as dialogue but as a monologue, a technical feature repeated throughout Tale 11—they aver the following:

>—Mucho crecen las nuevas   de mio Cid el
>   Campeador,
>bien casariemos con sus fijas   pora huebos de pro.
>Non la osariemos acometer   nós esta razón,
>mio Cid es de Bivar   e nós de los condesde
>   Carrión—
>Non lo dizen a nadi   e fincó esta razón.
>   (ll. 1373–77)
>["The prestige of My Cid the Battler is increasing
>   greatly;
>we would do well to marry his daughters for our
>   gain.
>We would not dare broach this affair,
>for My Cid is from Vivar and we are of the line of
>   Carrión."
>They told no one and the matter rested.]

Instead, they direct an inverted form of an interdiction (γ^2), a request, to the hero, in this case Minaya Álvar Fáñez. They bid him to give the Cid their regards and express their intention to favor the Cid whenever a situation allows them to do so. They suggest, also, that the Cid has nothing to lose by caring for them in return:

>Los ifantes de Carrión   [. . . . .]
>dando ivan compaña   a Minaya Álbar Fáñez:
>—En todo sodes pro,   en esto assí lo fagades:
>saludadnos   a mio Cid el de Bivar,
>somos en so pro   cuanto lo podemos far,
>el Cid que bien nos quiera   nada non perderá.—
>   (ll. 1385–1385*b*, ll. 1386–89)
>[The Infantes of Carrión rode out with Minaya Álvar
>   Fáñez:
>"You are obliging in all things, be so in this matter:

give our greetings to My Cid of Vivar,
we will both do for him all that we can.
If the Cid gives us his friendship it will not be to his
disadvantage."]

Minaya Álvar Fáñez, in turn, has no qualms about responding that he will comply with their petition (δ), since what they solicit is, apparently, a matter of little or no pragmatic consequence: "—Esto non me á por qué pesar—" (l. 1390) ["'This will be no trouble'"]. Or so it would appear. But appearances can be deceiving, and Minaya Álvar Fáñez's proleptic promise is, indeed, a misleading reply in this particular case. For upon his return to Valencia, Minaya Álvar Fáñez remains silent regarding what had transpired between the infantes and himself back in Carrión. Moreover, there is nothing in the text that supports or would even suggest that he, at this time, holds them in low esteem as a consequence of any of their past actions.

With Minaya Álvar Fáñez's above rejoinder to the infantes of Carrión, the exposition of this move ends. The development of the tale of the marriage of don Fernando and that of don Diego to doña Elvira and doña Sol continues with the arrival of Minaya Álvar Fáñez and Pedro Bermúdez in Valladolid bearing tributes for King Alfonso. (These are the prizes of war that the Cid obtained at the expense of the Moorish King Yúsuf, who left Morocco in a vain attempt to recover Valencia and other territories in the vicinity that formerly belonged to his domain [see Chapter 3, Tale 1: Move 15, and the Appendix].) Single and psychologically driven by a desire to augment constantly the material wealth of their estate ($a^{1,5}$), the infantes direct their attention to the daughters of the Cid. At this stage of the diegesis, the Cid's prodigious fortune must equal or possibly exceed that of King Alfonso. Hence the decision of don Fernando and don Diego to wed the daughters of the Cid rests not on affection but on material greed. Their interest is underscored below by the use of a consonant-paroxytone rhyme "emos" and an assonant-paroxytone rhyme "e-a": "—Las nuevas del Cid   mucho van adelant, / demandemos sus fijas   pora con ellas casar, / creçremos en nuestra ondra   e iremos adelant—" (ll. 1881–83) ["'For the Cid things are going very well; / let us ask for his daughters in marriage; / we shall grow in honour by it and so we shall prosper'"]. Thus motivated, the infantes immediately approach

King Alfonso and entreat him to intervene on their behalf and obtain for them the hands of the daughters of the Cid in marriage. The infantes underscore their brief deesis to King Alfonso by means of alliteration: "con" / "consejo" / "queremos" / "casar" / "queremos" / "con", and by their use of the assonant-paroxytone rhyme "e-o", which they repeat three times in line 1886:

—¡Merced vos pedimos commo a rey e a señor natural!
Con vuestro consejo lo queremos fer nós,
que nos demandedes fijas del Campeador;
casar queremos con ellas a su ondra e a nuestra pro.—" (ll. 1885–88)
["We ask a favour of you as our king and natural lord!
If you will grant your permission, we want you to ask on our behalf for the Battler's daughters in marriage;
we want to marry them, to their greater honour and our advantage."]

King Alfonso intuitively demurs to do their bidding. The narrator first communicates the king's initial state of apprehension in a consonant-oxytone rhyme of the vowel "o" ("pensó" / "comidió"), preceded by a parelcon included to emphasize the gravity of his concern ("Una grant ora"). Next, the narrator has the king express his state of uncertainty by having him stress the vowels "e" ("eché" / "tierra" / "buen" / "él" / "él" / "sé"), "a" ("mal" / "grand" / "abrá"), and "o" ("Yo" / "Campeador" / "yo" / "pro" / "non" / "sabor"), by his use of an assonant-paroxytone rhyme "e-o" ("faziendo" / "casamiento"), by having him acknowledge in a prozeugma and antithesis the wrong committed against the Cid and the latter's continued loyalty to his person: "e faziendo yo a él mal   e él a mí grand pro," and, finally, by having don Alfonso close his remarks with a paroemion in which the first letter of the last four words begin with the consonant "s" ("sé" / "si" / "s'abrá" / "sabor"):

Una grant ora el rey   pensó e comidió:
—Yo eché de tierra   al buen Campeador,
e faziendo yo a él mal   e él a mí grand pro,
del casamiento   non sé si s'abrá sabor.—
(ll. 1889–92)
[For a good hour the King thought and reflected
on this:
"I sent the good Battler into exile;
I have done him wrong and he has done me much
good,
and I do not know if he will be pleased by the
proposal of marriage."]

However, immediately thereafter, King Alfonso acquiesces to their petition: "—mas, pues bós lo queredes,   entremos en la razón—" (l. 1893) ["'But, since you wish it, let us discuss the matter'"]. Don Alfonso next orders both Minaya Álvar Fáñez and Pedro Bermúdez to act as his messengers and convey to the Cid that he wishes to meet with him, at a location of don Rodrigo's choosing, to discuss the marriage of doña Elvira and that of doña Sol to don Fernando and don Diego. (Note that this is the first time the text refers to the infantes by their Christian names.) The king avers (unknowingly and in error) that this event will benefit and honor the Cid (B). Don Alfonso's confident tone manifests itself through the monarch's use of a polyptoton ("onor" / "ondra"), a consonant-oxytone rhyme ("abrá" / "creçrá"), and an assonant-oxytone rhyme ("creçrá" / "consagrar") : "—abrá ý ondra   e creçrá en onor / por consagrar   con los ifantes de Carrión—" (ll. 1905–6) ["'He will gain honour and greater wealth / by becoming related to the Infantes of Carrión'"]. The Cid's two knights accept the contract and depart (C↑).

In Valencia Minaya Álvar Fáñez and Pedro Bermúdez assume the role of donors (D) in that they diligently communicate to the Cid the message entrusted to them by King Alfonso. Although not pleased with the prospect of having the infantes of Carrión as his sons-in-law (their excessive pride deeply troubles him), don Rodrigo finally accedes to the king's invitation to meet to discuss the marriage of his daughters to don Fernando and don Diego (E):

69

> —Ellos son mucho urgullosos e an part en la cort;
> d'este casamiento non avría sabor,
> mas, pues lo conseja el que más vale que nós,
> fablemos en ello, en la poridad seamos nós.—
> (ll. 1938–41)
> ["They are very proud and powerful members of the court;
> I would not agree to this marriage,
> but, since it is proposed by one worth more than us,
> let us talk of this matter, and let us do so in private."]

In a connective link (§) the Cid sends a letter to the king indicating the banks of the Tajo River as the meeting place; the king determines that the meeting will take place in three weeks. At the appointed time King Alfonso and the infantes of Carrión, with a large entourage, traverse terrains on horseback and reach their destination one day before the Cid arrives ($\uparrow G^2$).

Here, the narrator intercalates four extensive segmental interludes before don Rodrigo and don Alfonso grapple over the question of whether this particular time is suitable for doña Elvira and doña Sol to wed don Fernando and don Diego. He lists the names of the knights who will accompany the Cid; he summarizes the Cid's order that no one is either to leave or enter Valencia during his absence; he relates that the king leaves his camp to greet the Cid upon hearing of the latter's approach; and he presents a vivid mimetic scene in which King Alfonso pardons the Cid and accepts him as his vassal (see Chapter 3, Tale 1. Move 16).

The next morning, following mass, the principals begin the discussion that has brought them together by the banks of the River Tajo. Don Alfonso officially proposes a difficult task to don Rodrigo, namely, that he give his daughters in marriage to the infantes (M). The emphatic tone of King Alfonso's illocutionary statement derives from his use of a polyptoton ("pido" / "piden"), three assonant-oxytone rhymes ("fijas" / "Elvira"; "dedes" / "mugieres"; "casamiento" / "ellos"), and a closing alliteration of the vowel "o" ("mándovoslo yo"), which the king purposely matches with his closing assonant-oxytone rhyme of his discourse of four lines ("Sol" / "Carrión" / "pro" / "yo"):

—¡Oídme, las escuelas,   cuendes e ifançones!
             Cometer quiero un ruego   a mio Cid el
                                                 Campeador,
             assí lo mande Christus   que sea a so pro:
             vuestras fijas vos pido,   don Elvira e doña Sol,
             que las dedes por mugieres a los ifantes de
                                                 Carrión.
             Seméjam' el casamiento   ondrado e con grant
                                                 pro,
             ellos vos las piden   e mándovoslo yo.—
                                                 (ll. 2072–78)
["Hear me, my courtiers, counts and lords!
I wish to make a request of My Cid the Battler;
may Christ ensure that it brings advantage!
I ask you to give your daughters, Doña Elvira and
                                      Doña Sol,
as wives to the Infantes of Carrión.
I consider the marriage to be honourable and to
                                      bring great prestige;
the Infantes ask it of you and I command it."]

    Interestingly, the scene that ensues between King Alfonso and don Rodrigo constitutes a mirrow-image doubling of that held previously between don Alfonso and the two brothers of Carrión. As in the above related scene of don Alfonso and don Fernando and don Diego, it is the Cid who, now, also demurs at first. Don Rodrigo, searching for an excuse that will extricate him from this unpleasant state of affairs, avers that his daughters are too young to enter into a marital relationship. He emphatically attempts to underscore the latter point by his use of an assonant-paroxytone rhyme "i-a" and an assonant-oxytone rhyme stressing the vowel "a": "—Non habría fijas de casar   —repuso el Campeador—, / ca non han grant edad   e de días pequeñas son—" (ll. 2082–83) ["'I would not have my daughters marry,' replied the Battler, / 'for they are still girls, young in years'"]. Unsuccessful in his endeavor, as it had been in the prior case with King Alfonso, don Rodrigo, as don Alfonso before him, acquiesces. He does so, however, once he convinces both King Alfonso to assume full responsibility for this marriage and Minaya Álvar Fáñez to consent to hand doña Elvira and doña Sol over to the infantes of Carrión at the wedding that will transpire at the abode of the Cid (N w[1]).[1] Next, the narrator introduces a coda. In this segmental interlude, the Cid tenders his presents to the king. Don Rodrigo underscores the quantity and quality of his gifts by means of two consonant-paroxytone rhymes ("einta" and "éstos"), one assonant-paroxytone rhyme ("a-o"), and by the use of the figures prozeugma (of the conjugated verb "tráyovos") and two isocolons ("treinta palafrés" / "treinta cavallos"; "bien adobados" / "bien ensellados"): "—tráyovos treinta palafrés,   éstos bien adobados, / e treinta cavallos corredores,   éstos bien ensellados—" (ll. 2144–45) ["'I have brought you twenty palfreys—these well equipped— / and thirty chargers—these well saddled'"]. The latter brings closure to their meeting. Adding the infantes of Carrión to his entourage, the Cid takes his leave of King Alfonso and, veering in an antithetical direction to that of his sovereign, don Rodrigo departs for Valencia (↓).

Move 2 (Cantar II)
The diegesis of Move 2 deals with the wedding of don Fernando and don Diego to doña Elvira and doña Sol. The symbolic transcription of this brief move is as follows:

aB:CDEFW*

(The above symbolic transcription corresponds to the numerical functions: VIIIa, IX, X, XII, XIII, XIV, XXXI, and a closing narratorial segmental statement in the form of an epilogue.)

The narrator, in an apostrophe to the reader that also constitutes a telescoping of space and a foreshortening of time, has the Cid and his entourage filing into Valencia immediately after they have taken their leave of King Alfonso: "Afelos en Valencia,   la que mio Cid gañó" (l. 2175) ["Here they are in Valencia, won by My Cid"]. Amidst his family, don Rodrigo declares in an illocutionary statement, which regrettably will fail to materialize, that the prospective tie to the González family will immediately confer great honor to the Díaz name (a): "—d'este vustro casamiento   creçremos en onor—" (l. 2198) ["'by these marriages our honour will grow'"]. His daughters' reaction, as the reader might surmise, is one of joy: "—¡Cuando vós nos casáredes   bien seremos ricas!—" (l. 2195) {"'When you will marry us <to the infantes of Carrión> we shall indeed acquire <the rank of> nobility!'"}. Perturbed by his daughters' state of euphoria at this unforeseen and sudden rise in aristocratic prestige, don Rodrigo is quick to point out to them the reservation and apprehension he harbors regarding the upcoming wedding. Interestingly, the Cid eliminates himself as a responsible agent of this union between his daughters and the infantes of Carrión by his clever use of the stressed vowel "o" in lines 2201–2 ("todo coraçón" / "yo" / "cosa" / "no" / "sope" / "no"):

—Mas bien sabet verdat, que non lo levanté yo:
pedidas vos ha e rogadas el mio señor Alfonso
atán firmemientre e de todo coraçón
que yo nulla cosa no l' sope dezir de no.—
(ll. 2199–2202)
["But you must know that they were not brought
about by me;
my lord, Alfonso, sought and asked for you,
so earnestly and so much from the heart,
that I could in no way oppose his command."]

To underscore further his fundamental and radical feeling of disapproval about what is to transpire, the Cid, by his use of alliteration—of the consonant sounds "m" and "k"—forthrightly declares King Alfonso solely responsible for the present state of affairs (B): "—Metívos en sus manos,   fijas amas a dos; / bien me lo creades   que él vos casa, ca non yo—" (ll. 2203–4) ["'I placed you both in his hands, my daughters. / You should realize that he, and not I, offers you in marriage'"].

The next morning, after all have gathered at the palace of the Cid, don Rodrigo publicly announces that, in compliance with the dictates of the arrangement agreed upon by the king, he is placing his daughters in the hands of Minaya Álvar Fáñez, his nephew, and orders his nephew to give his daughters to the infantes to be their wives (B). Minaya Álvar Fáñez complies, and in so doing combines two functions: namely, that of hero and donor (CD). In turn, each infante, upon receiving his respective wife, assumes the function of the reaction of the hero (EF). It is important to note that the narrator goes out of his way to underscore that the infantes do so willingly, with pleasure, with love: "Amos las reciben   d'amor e de grado" (l. 2234) ["They both received them with love and pleasure"]. This diegetic fact creates a serious structural problem for the reader when he or she subsequently endeavors to reconcile the positive affective state of the infantes in this passage with the subsequent vicious comportment of don Fernando and don Diego toward their wives at Corpes.

Following the religious ceremony of said wedding in the Santa María Church, festivities celebrating the above event run for a period of fifteen days (W*).[2] To conclude with what is relevant to this move, the narrator apprises the reader in an aside or epilogue, another passage of spatial and temporal foreshortening, that the guests from Castile have returned to their estates and that the two married couples have lived, to the contentment of the Cid and his vassals, in a harmonious state for nearly two years. The narrator underscores the latter not only by his use of the assonant-paroxytone rhymes of "a-e" and "e-a", but also by the figures polyptoton ("eran" / "era") and prozeugma (of the conjugated verb "era")—in passing, this prozeugma immediately transforms itself into a syllepsis ("alegre era el Cid   e todos sus vassallos")—: "Ý moran los ifantes   bien cerca de dos años, / los amores que les fazen   mucho eran sobejanos; / alegre era el Cid   e todos sus vassallos" (ll. 2271–73) ["There the Infantes stayed for almost two years, / and great indeed was the love lavished upon them. / Joyful were the Cid and all his vassals"]. Unless the narrator changes the diegetic direction of his work at this point, this epic poem, enveloped in joy and harmony, has come to a complete stop.

Or at least it would so appear. At this juncture, the reader of the *Cantar de Mio Cid* must ask whether the epic poem can come to rest. It is evident that the narrator, with respect to Rodrigo Díaz of Vivar, has not framed his epic poem within the mode of tragedy. That is, the narrator has not depicted an individual who starts in an elevated socio-political position of privilege, enjoying all the material amenities of prosperity and the corresponding affective state of happiness that such external caste-rank provides, and concluding with the same individual experiencing a crashing fall from grace, a fall that aetiologically is based on a serious character flaw, in which he loses not only his prestige, but his economic affluence, as well. In the Cid's case, just the opposite holds true. This case is one in which a man has gone from rags to riches, progressively rising in social class and economic affluence, a scenario that definitely pertains to the mode of comedy. As the reader of the *Cantar de Mio Cid* will recall, the epic poem opens with the Cid's fall from King Alfonso's grace; continues with the Cid's conquest of Moorish lands, from whose inhabitants he receives monetary tributes; and concludes, thus far, with his taking possession of Valencia and its surrounding areas. From a pragmatic perspective, the latter achievement has substantially filled the Cid's coffers with gold and silver, a treasury of seemingly inexhaustible funds. More importantly, it has provided him with a kingly fief wherein he exercises absolute power—so absolute, in fact, that the Cid feels no pangs of hubris in marrying off the ladies-in-waiting of his wife and of his daughters to vassals under his command, a social act that falls within the exclusive province of a monarch. Finally, the marriage of doña Elvira and that of doña Sol to the infantes of Carrión attest to don Rodrigo's advancement in social status. By marrying his daughters to the members of the González family, the Cid has linked his family to one of the oldest families in Spain whose noble lineage, thus far, has remained unblemished. With respect to the marriages of doña Elvira and doña Sol to don Fernando and don Diego, it should be underscored that both don Rodrigo and his vassals joyfully celebrate the newly achieved state of civil, marital, and domestic felicity.

  The above charged atmosphere of joy, love, and peace suggests that closure of the epic poem might be possible at the end of Move 2. Why does the omniscient first-person narrator intentionally intervene at this point to startle his reader, whom he has lulled into a quiescent state of lethargy, with the following ecphonetic deesis: "¡Plega a Santa María e al Padre Santo / que s' pague d'es casamiento mio Cid o el que lo ovo a algo!" (ll. 2274–75) ["May it please Saint Mary and the Holy Father / that My Cid, and the man who valued him so highly, should gain joy from this wedding!"]? Why does he add: "¡Las coplas d'este cantar aquí s' van acabando, / el Criador vos vala con todos los sos santos!" (ll. 2276–77) ["Now the verses of this song are coming to an end; / may the Creator, with all his saints, protect you!"]? Why does he not state, instead, "the verses of this (epic) poem are coming to an end"?

  Clearly, the narrator's objective is to advert his reader that the poem has not concluded with the created universe of serene harmony in Move 2. The question remains then: Why has the narrator bothered to use this device? For the attentive reader of this epic, the exclamatory words of indirection are both intrusive and unwarranted. Indeed, the narrator's ecphonesis-deesis constitutes a variant of the figure parelcon, a superfluous addition of words, which, from a structural point of view, he need not have intercalated. It is by fault of analepsis that the narrator here defaults on his ontologic role of omniscience—that is, the narrator has forgotten the scene of dramatic irony in Move 1 that had provided his reader with privileged information regarding don Fernando's and don Diego's aetiological interest in doña Elvira and doña Sol. The reader is privy to the knowledge, withheld from the other actants in the *Cantar de Mio Cid*, that an unceasing, near-fanatical materialistic compulsion to accumulate wealth had originally predicated the interest of the infantes of Carrión in the daughters of the Cid.

With this in mind, it is patent that the narrator cannot bring closure to the epic poem at the end of Move 2. To do so would make a mockery of the principled character and behavior of the Cid. In fact, it would reduce to ridicule everything that don Rodrigo had stood for thus far in the narrative. Closure of the epic poem at this point would relegate to persiflage questions regarding ethical principles of conduct. It would allow for calculated, sophisticated, intellectual fraud to trump purity of moral comportment. Closure at this point would establish, also, the sovereignty of Satan's unbridled pursuit of evil over God's conception of life founded on righteousness and reason. If the narrator were to take this option, he would abandon his reader in the mire of immorality, advocating that he become a follower of the Antichrist. He would deride, in effect, the views expressed up to this point in his narratorial voice and those voiced by don Rodrigo and doña Jimena, of the need for an individual to lead a Christian life, of the imperative that one put one's trust in God. (For instance, consider the narrator's rendition of doña Jimena's devotional deesis to safeguard her husband during the period of his exile in lines 330–65.) Hence, the narrator must reverse the idyllic state that don Fernando and don Diego enjoy for such a triumphant life founded on greed lacks moral sense. Since the narrator has made cupidity the fundamental driving force in don Fernando's and don Diego's lives, their fall and their exclusion from orderly society must also be derived from their avidity. Instead, the narrator subterfuges the artistic design of his epic poem by choosing two actions that bear no relation to the motif of greed to debase don Fernando and don Diego. Structurally ill-conceived schemes, both of these diegetic incidents reveal a serious aesthetic flaw of the *Cantar de Mio Cid*. As for the first of the two events of meiosis that initiates the deconstruction of don Fernando's and don Diego's esteem in the eyes of the Cid's vassals—namely, that of the loose lion event in Move 3 below—it constitutes a deus ex machina occurrence that lacks grounding in any heretofore reported diegetic event.

Move 3 (Cantar III)

This narrative deals with a loose lion incident that appears to place the life of the Cid in peril and reveals a serious character flaw of the infantes of Carrión. From a structural point of view, this episode is redundant. The symbolic transcription of this brief move is as follows:

$$aBC-H-\{M\}JI-\{N-\}K^4-$$

(The above symbolic transcription corresponds to the numerical functions: VIIIa, IX, X, XVI, {XXV}, XVII, XVIII {XXVI}, and XIX.)

The basic function of this move is the disclosure of don Fernando and don Diego as cowards. Based on this meiosis, their roles in the epic poem change from protagonists to that of unmitigated antagonists. Were they to plunge from their station based on a character flaw not founded on evil, then the fate of the infantes of Carrión would fall within the mode of tragedy. As tragic figures they would constitute an antithetical foil to the Cid. For as the Cid rises from poverty to material affluence, acquiring in the process military fame, social prestige, and political power, the infantes of Carrión, in contrast, lose the favor of King Alfonso, find their prestige reduced among their noble peers, and see their economic condition significantly deteriorate. However, as I have stated above, don Fernando and don Diego cannot evolve into tragic figures because they personify intractable greed. Hence, from a structural point of view, their prospective fall must result from their unbridled and all-consuming greed that drives them to acquire new wealth. The fact that the reversal of their fortune does not stem from their aforementioned greed constitutes a serious aesthetic flaw of the *Cantar de Mio Cid.*

Before delving into an analysis of Move 3, I should point out that there are two reasons why the lion incident constitutes a deus ex machina diegetic segment. The first reason is that nothing in the Cid's past actions warrants that his present conduct should be that of an eccentric, ostentatious, and vain person; one who needs to flaunt his wealth by acquiring an exotic beast of prey. The second reason is that nothing at this point in this epic poem sets the necessary and sufficient grounds to justify the future comportment of the infantes as pusillanimous individuals. With the above critical frame in place, the analysis of Move 3 can now commence.

Cantar III begins with the narrator addressing his reader in an apostrophe, notifying her or him that a lion on the house premises has managed to escape from his cage and that the king of beasts stands not too far from the bench where presently the king of Spanish warriors lies peacefully asleep: "Yaziés' en un escaño,   durmié el Campeador; / mala sobrevienta   sabed que les cuntió: / saliós' de la red   e desatós' el león" (ll. 2280–82) ["Lying on a couch, the Battler slept; / the Infantes, I tell you, had a terrible shock: / the lion broke free and escaped from his cage"]. Whereas the vassals of the Cid rush to encircle don Rodrigo in order to protect him, don Fernando and don Diego, who are present, as well, rush to escape in an egotistical fit of self-preservation. The conduct of the infantes reveals to the Cid's retinue their psychological state of despair, panic, and their lack of courage (a). Don Fernando, finding no place to hide, thrusts himself under don Rodrigo's bench: "metiós' so l'escaño" (l. 2287) ["hid under the couch"]. Meanwhile, don Diego, pathetically clamoring that he will never again see his beloved estate in Carrión (B): "—¡Non veré Carrión!—" (l. 2289) ["'Never again shall I see Carrión!'"], hides behind a winepress. Thus, these two antagonists, these two antiheroes (C-), refuse to confront the lion. Their behavior constitutes a negative rendition of function XVI: they do not engage in a direct struggle with a villain (H-). (Here function XVI assimilates function XXV: a difficult task {M}.) Moreover, by hiding behind a winepress, don Diego unwittingly allows the dregs from wine making to soil his garments, an occurrence that, in a decidedly peculiar manner, marks him (J): "el manto e el brial   todo suzio lo sacó" (l. 2291) {"his cloak and tunic were all soiled"}.[3] Thus it is clear that the infantes do not overcome the lion (I-). Here function XVIII assimilates the negative aspect of function XXVI, namely, that the infantes do not resolve their difficult task {N-}—and so they fail to erase the stigma of cowardice that the Cid's knights now associate with the names of the two brothers of Carrión. Indeed, the Cid's subsequent order to those in his court that they cease in their criticism and ridicule of don Fernando and don Diego over the lion affair: "mandólo vedar mio Cid el Campeador" (l. 2308) ["My Cid the Battler forbade it to continue"], serves not to resolve but to highlight further the crisis that his two sons-in-law have created for themselves by having exposed themselves in public as pusillanimous individuals (K^4-).[4]

The above closing circumstance of Move 3 creates an interesting diegetic situation. Can don Fernando and don Diego take their leave of the Cid and of Valencia after this incident and return to their estate in Carrión with their wives, erasing, somehow, the affair of the lion from their minds? The narrative implications of such an occurrence would have constituted another embarrassing and humiliating spectacle for both don Fernando and don Diego. At this point, they would be forever remembered and judged as having been driven into retreat by the derision of the inhabitants of Valencia. At this point, moreover, it is unlikely that the Cid would allow his daughters to depart from Valencia. To consent to such a move on the Cid's part would completely erase the hard-earned prestige of don Rodrigo and eternally envelop him in ridicule before all the nobles of Spain. It would signal to the infantes that he would condone their mistreatment, their battering of doña Elvira and doña Sol, and even possibly their murder. What other means would be available to the infantes to expunge their suppressed, albeit not psychologically repressed, bitterness engendered by the reaction of the Cid's vassals in this affair of the lion than by violently unleashing their pent-up spite against their wives? At this juncture of the diegesis, were doña Elvira and doña Sol to flee with their husbands to Carrión, it is likely that their parents, along with the vassals of the Cid, would judge their self-imposed exile from Valencia as an act of ignominy. How else could one interpret such a disgraceful departure? In their exile, how could doña Elvira and doña Sol retain their respect for their husbands? The despicable conduct of don Fernando and don Diego during the lion incident would remain fresh in the minds of doña Elvira and doña Sol. If dragged into exile, the daughters of don Rodrigo would be repelled, if not downright disgusted, by the prospect of sharing the remaining years of their existence with the infantes who, because of their abandonment of the Cid for the sake of their own survival, now symbolically represent the filth of mankind.

Moreover, the narrator is clearly focused on didactically proving that an individual's merit does not lie in one's inherited lineage; rather, merit lies in the ethical, moral, and religious values that an individual not only professes, but also applies in his pragmatic, everyday social intercourse with his fellow human beings. Regrettably, the narrator has figuratively boxed himself in by marrying egregiously scandalous scoundrels of noble descent to the daughters of a fine military knight who is, at the same time, an exemplar of the Christian faith. At this point of the diegesis it is structurally impossible for the infantes to remain in Valencia. Were they to do so, the Cid, his court, his vassals, and the infantes themselves, would be forced to conduct their daily existence in a constant state of duplicity and hypocrisy. Therefore, the question arises: How will the narrator extricate himself from this self-created dilemma in order to permit don Fernando and don Diego to save face so as to allow them, with a modicum of dignity, to depart from the Cid's side and from Valencia? The answer: with some difficulty. The narrator's diegetic handling of this issue to be discussed below constitutes Move 4 of the tale of the two brothers of Carrión.

Move 4 (Cantar III)

In this move the narrator provides a diegetic rendition of the military stand of don Fernando and don Diego against the Moroccan King Búcar and his forces, who cross the Mediterranean Sea to lay siege to Valencia. This part of the narrative, with respect to the role that the infantes of Carrión play in this battle, is somewhat ambiguous. (Regarding King Búcar, the narrator in a structural miscue suggests in an apostrophe that his reader possibly has heard of him: "Aqueste era el rey Bucar, si l'oviestes contar" [l. 2314] ["This was the Emir Búcar; perhaps you have heard tell of him"], an unreasonable fictive diegetic assumption since the narrator has never mentioned this king's name before in his narrative epic poem.) Before proceeding, one should note that the King Búcar episode constitutes, from an immediate perspective, another gratuitous narrative about the need of the Cid to prove once more his valor and his merit as a military campaign strategist and defender of Valencia. His resounding victory over the Moroccan King Yúsuf firmly established his valor once and for all. Why, then, does the narrator intercalate this episode at this juncture? I suggest that the narrator introduces this episode at this point of his epic poem for two structural purposes. First, the narrator needs to demean further the figures of don Fernando and don Diego. He must show that their cowardice is a major character flaw of the infantes and not just a passing occurrence so that their social acceptance within the fold of the Cid's exclusive society of meritorious men becomes an unattainable goal. (In turn, such exclusion would effectively eliminate the political, military, and social role of the infantes in Valencia and foster in them a resolve to return to Carrión, where their dominion is absolute.) The second reason is that the narrator must, paradoxically, elevate the stature of don Fernando and don Diego to some degree so that if they were to express a desire to return to Carrión with their wives, the Cid would lack a legitimate reason not to comply with their request. The narrator's job is a difficult one, indeed. He succeeds in his objectives, but he does so with great difficulty.

The symbolic transcription of Move 4 is as follows:

$$aB: \{ \underline{C} \uparrow: \underline{H^1\text{-}I^1}\text{-} K^4\text{-}L\}\downarrow:K^4L::\text{-}w^o$$
$$\{ C \uparrow H \quad I^1 \}$$

(The above symbolic transcription corresponds to the numerical functions: VIIIa, IX, {X, XI, XVI, XVIII, XIX, XXIV}, XX, XIX, XXIV, and XXXI.)

The opening narrative scene of Move 4 describes the fifty thousand tents that the Moorish King Búcar and his forces have set up in their siege of Valencia. The narrator's undisguised use of the hyperbole here serves to set off the despair of the infantes of Carrión. Don Fernando's and don Diego's reaction marks still another instance of their cowardly disposition and exemplifies their apparent dedication to the creed of self-preservation (a). The infantes engage in an intimate dialogue in which they assume that death is inevitable, woefully lament the fact that they will never again set foot in Carrión, and sentimentally bewail the future widowhood of their wives:

—Catamos la ganancia   e la pérdida no.
Ya en esta batalla   a entrar abremos nós,
esto es aguisado   por non ver Carrión,
bibdas remandrán   fijas del Campeador.—
(ll. 2320–23)
["We are looking for gains; we do not wish for
losses;
now we shall have to enter this battle;

>   this may well mean that we shall never see Carrión
>   again.
>   The Battler's daughters will be left widows."]

To advance the diegesis of these two brothers, the narrator provides a deus ex machina passage where Muño Gustioz overhears their conversation. (Muño Gustioz, in an unlikely situation, would need to have been unobserved at their side to understand the words uttered by the brothers in such an intimate and low voice.) The Cid's vassal immediately reports the brothers' conversation to the Cid. Following his disclosure, Muño Gustioz advises the Cid to keep his sons-in-law in the palace while the rest go forth to do battle with the Moors (B):

>   —¡Evades qué pavor han vuestros yernos,   tan
>   osados son,
>   por entrar en batalla   desean Carrión!
>   Idlos conortar,   sí vos vala el Criador,
>   que sean en paz   e non ayan ý ración.—
>   (ll. 2326–29)
>   ["Look at the fear of your sons-in-law; they are so
>   bold
>   at the thought of going into battle that they long for
>   Carrión!
>   Go and give them encouragement, may the Creator
>   protect you!
>   Let them be at ease and not take part in the battle."]

The Cid takes the above advice to heart and counsels both don Fernando and don Diego to remain with his daughters within the palace grounds (B):

>   —¡Dios vos salve, yernos,   ifantes de Carrión!
>   En braços tenedes mis fijas,   tan blancas commo
>   el sol.
>   Yo desseo lides   e vós a Carrión;
>   en Valencia folgad   a todo vuestro sabor,
>   ca d'aquellos moros   yo só sabidor,

arrancármelos trevo   con la merced del
                          Criador.— (ll. 2332–37)
["May God watch over you, my sons-in-law,
                             Infantes of Carrión!
You are married to my daughters, as white as the
                                                sun.
I long for battle, you for Carrión.
Rest in Valencia at your pleasure,
for I know those Moors well.
I am brave enough to defeat them, with the
                             Creator's blessing!"]

There are several lines missing after line 2337. (An episode similar to the one described above, including the same cast of actants, appears in the *Crónica de Veinte Reyes*. In this chronicle, the infantes of Carrión request the Cid to allow them to be the first to engage the enemy in battle. Accordingly, don Fernando ventures forth in the company of Pedro Bermúdez to duel with a Moor {C↑}, but subsequently flees out of fear {H¹-I¹-}. After killing the Moor, Pedro Bermúdez gives the Moor's horse to don Fernando so that he may falsely claim the death of the Moor as his deed of accomplishment [Menéndez Pidal, *Poema de Mio Cid* 230–31].) The *Cantar de Mio Cid* resumes with Fernando's words of gratitude, which refer to the issue mentioned in the above parenthetical commentary: "—Aún vea el ora   que vos meresca dos tanto—" (l. 2338) ["'May the time come when I repay this twice over'"], and with the narrator informing his reader that Pedro Bermúdez later confirms don Fernando's false claim of having slain the Moor before the Cid and his knights ({K⁴-L}): "Assí lo otorga don Pero   cuemo se alaba Ferrando" (l. 2340) ["Don Pedro confirmed Fernando's boastful claims"].

Following Pedro Bermúdez's words, nothing next transpires in the epic poem with respect to the infantes of Carrión. The narrator, however, purposely intervenes to disclose information that puts don Fernando and don Diego in a very poor light. Amidst the blasting noise of the drums of the Moors announcing the next stage of the battle, the narrator avers that the infantes "por la su voluntad   non serién allí llegados" (l. 2349) ["would never have been there of their own desire"]. Also, he has the Cid communicate his desire to protect his sons-in-law to Pedro Bermúdez, who begs off from serving as their shield (lines 2351–57). These negative factors regarding the infantes of Carrión, however, promptly dissipate. In the segments below, the narrator, don Rodrigo, and Minaya Álvar Fáñez will refer to don Fernando and don Diego in positive terms. After the defeat of the Moors, don Fernando and don Diego, who during the battle against the forces of King Búcar had vanished from the pages of the epic poem, reappear on the scene. At court, the Cid lauds his sons-in-law for their military valor.[5, 6] His paeanismus emphatically underscores the social regeneration of the infantes of Carrión and the very positive esteem in which the Cid presently holds both don Fernando and don Diego. Don Rodrigo's words highlight the fact that his sons-in-law have participated in the battle against the forces of the Moorish King Búcar with honor and valor: ($\{C\uparrow H^1 I^1\}$ K^4L-): "—¡Venides, mios yernos, mios fijos sodes amos! / Sé que de lidiar   bien sodes pagados, / a Carrión de vós   irán buenos mandados—" (ll. 2443–45) ["'It is you, my sons-in-law! You are as sons to me! / I know that you have taken pleasure in the battle; / good reports will go to Carrión of you'"]. At this point, Minaya Álvar Fáñez makes his entrance and reconfirms the Cid's impression that the infantes, in effect, have shown their mettle in combat (K^4L-): "—e vuestros yernos   aquí son ensayados, / fartos de lidiar con moros en el campo—" (ll. 2460–61) ["'Your sons-in-law have proved themselves here, / and are tired now with fighting against Moors on the field of battle'"]. The words uttered by the Cid's nephew, in turn, elicit the following brief comment from the Cid: "—Yo d'esto só pagado, / cuando agora son buenos   adelant serán preciados—" (ll. 2462–63) ["'With this I am pleased. / They are now fine men—in future [*sic*] they will be even more highly esteemed'"].

What follows are four segmental interludes, which appear toward the close of Move 4. Their function is to reiterate, and thus reinforce, the above positive attributes assigned to don Fernando and don Diego by don Rodrigo and Minaya Álvar Fáñez. The Cid, at a subsequent palace function, unequivocally states that both don Fernando and don Diego fought valiantly against the Moors at his side:

> Grant fue el día   en la cort del Campeador,
> después que esta batalla vencieron   e al rey Bucar
>   mató.

> Alçó la mano, a la barba se tomó:
> —¡Grado a Christus, que del mundo es señor,
> cuando veo lo que avía sabor,
> que lidiaran conmigo en campo mios yernos
> amos a dos!
> Mandados buenos irán d'ellos a Carrión,
> cómmo son ondrados e avervos han grant pro.—
> (ll. 2474-81)
> [It was a great day in the court of the Battler,
> since they had won this battle and My Cid had killed
> the Emir Búcar.
> My Cid raised his hand, and held his beard:
> "Thanks be to Christ, who is Lord of the world,
> for now I see what I have desired,
> that my two sons-in-law have fought at my side on
> the field of battle.
> Good reports of them will go to Carrión,
> telling of how they have won honour, and we shall
> gain great advantage by it."]

Next, the omniscient narrator, whose view is incontrovertible, readily corroborates the previous assertions that the Cid and Minaya Álvar Fáñez averred (K^4L-): "Grandes son los gozos de sus yernos amos a dos, / d'aquesta arrancada que lidiaron de coraçón / valía de cinco mill marcos ganaron amos a dos" (ll. 2507-9) ["Great is the joy of his two sons-in-law; / for, from this victorious battle which they had fought with all their heart / both of them had won booty worth five thousand marks"]. The third affirmative reiteration of the valor of the infantes of Carrión comes from Minaya Álvar Fáñez, stated at a subsequent courtly function (K^4L-): "—¡Acá venid, cuñados, que más valemos por vós!—" (l. 2517) ["'Come here, my brothers-in-law; you have increased our prestige!'"]. The last comment is that of the Cid. Espying them after they enter the court, he receives them with jubilation. His paeanismus emphatically underscores the regeneration of don Fernando and don Diego and reveals that he holds his two sons-in-law in very high esteem (K^4L-):

> Assí commo llegaron,　　pagós' el Campeador:
> —Evades aquí, yernos,　　la mi mugier de pro
> e amas las mis fijas,　　don Elvira e doña Sol,
> bien vos abracen　　e sírvanvos de coraçón.
> ¡Grado a Santa María,　　madre del nuestro señor Dios,
> d'estos vuestros casamientos　　vós abredes honor,
> buenos mandados irán　　a tierras de Carrión!—
> 　　　　　　　　　　　　　　　　(ll. 2518–26)
> [At their arrival, the Battler was well pleased:
> "Here, my sons-in-law, is my worthy wife,
> and here are my two daughters, Doña Elvira and
> 　　　　　　　　　　　　　　　　Doña Sol;
> they are to embrace you warmly and serve you
> 　　　　　　　　　　　　　　　　faithfully.
> Thanks be to Saint Mary, the Mother of our Lord
> 　　　　　　　　　　　　　　　　God!
> From your marriages you will gain honour,
> and good reports will go to the lands of Carrión"]

Regarding the economic outcome of the war against King Búcar, the Cid and his vassals have profited greatly. In turn, don Fernando and don Diego have received five thousand marks as their share, a sum sufficient to secure their well-being forever (w°): "cuidaron que en sus días nuncua serién minguados" (l. 2470) ["<they> thought that in all their days they would never be in need"]; "mucho's' tienen por ricos los ifantes de Carrión" (l. 2510) ["The Infantes of Carrión thought themselves very wealthy men"].

From the above, it is evident that the narrator has remedied, by and large, the serious defect referring to the lack of courage that the infantes had exhibited in the lion incident. Namely, he has sufficiently raised the esteem of don Fernando and don Diego to counteract their flaw, at least in his eyes and in those of Minaya Álvar Fáñez and don Rodrigo. At this juncture, the infantes have no obligation to remain with the Cid in Valencia. Quite the contrary is the case. With their prestige restored, they are at the zenith of their material prosperity and the apex of their political power in Valencia. Since the Cid has not indicated a willingness to transfer his political dominion over Valencia and its environs to the infantes, don Fernando and don Diego could now justifiably retire with their wives to their estate in Carrión. Were they to make this request, the Cid would have to comply with their wishes, finding no serious excuse warranting his denial.

However, there is an aesthetic weakness in the apparent gain of the infantes. The omniscient first-person narrator succinctly and abstractly tells the reader of their participation in the military conflict against King Búcar and his Moorish forces. That is, he prefers to communicate to the reader the indirect judgments leveled at don Fernando and don Diego, not only by the Cid and Minaya Álvar Fáñez, but also by his own person. What the narrator fails to do is to provide his reader with an objective correlative to substantiate such meritorious, illocutionary assertions. In other words, the narrator never shows the infantes distinguishing themselves as warriors in a dramatic battle scene, behavior that would convince the reader that don Fernando and don Diego have effectively overcome their original flaw of cowardice.

The aesthetic flaw regarding the infantes of Carrión constitutes an act of proairesis on the narrator's part to inhibit his readers from deliberately responding too favorably to don Fernando and don Diego. To demonstrate that he has absolute control over his reader's response to the text, the narrator will go out of his way shortly to undermine, once more, the status of don Fernando and don Diego. Regardless, Move 4 closes on a positive note. At the very least, the infantes have redeemed themselves in the eyes of the Cid and in those of Minaya Álvar Fáñez and of the narrator. Furtheremore, as a reward for their military participation against King Búcar, they are at present exceedingly affluent. The negative aspect alluded to above, sets the background for Move 5.

Move 5 (Cantar III)
Move 5 details the infantes' departure from Valencia to return to Carrión.

Below is the backdrop to Move 5. During a gathering at the Cid's palace to celebrate the victory over the Moorish army under the command of King Búcar, the Cid warmly and graciously embraces don Fernando and don Diego with words as sweet as wine (see lines 2518–26 in Move 4). In turn, don Fernando replies in a surprising and disquieting manner. His words neither refer to the infantes' beloved wives nor to the wife of the Cid—the three women, in fact, seem not to exist for him. Rather he indulges in self-gratifying praise, in vainglory. He stresses that he and his brother participated in defeating the Moors and then continues falsely to claim that they killed King Búcar: "—venciemos moros en campo e matamos / a aquel rey Bucar, traidor provado—" (ll. 2522–23) ["'<we> defeated Moors on the field of battle and killed / the renowned Emir Búcar, a proven traitor'"]. His words, the narrator remarks, give rise to telling smiles among the Cid's knights who, according to the narrator, never saw the infantes engaged in any dangerous or significant military encounter with the Moors: "Vasallos de mio Cid seyénse sonrisando / quién lidiara mejor o quién fuera en alcanço, / mas non fallavan ý a Diego ni a Ferrando" (ll. 2532–34) ["At this My Cid's vassals smiled; / some had been the best of the fighters and others had gone in pursuit, / but they had not found Diego or Fernando among them"].[7]

The narrator's intervention above in lines 2532–34, as well as in lines 2535–36 ("Por aquestos juegos que ivan levantando / e las noches e los días tan mal los escarmentando" ["As a result of the mockery which now began among the men, / by night and by day teaching the Infantes so cruel a lesson"]), marks a deus ex machina instance that drives the action forward. This development, in which the Cid's vassals again deride and disdain don Fernando and don Diego, provokes the infantes to loathe those in the Cid's court and to force the infantes to take action that will remove them from the court's presence, severing their ties to the Cid and Valencia. The irony is that lines 2532–34 and lines 2535–36 are structurally unnecessary. The infantes have regained their social respectability by their courageous participation in the battle against the Moors. Economically, the infantes have satisfied many times over their desire for material wealth. However, their political advancement in Valencia has come to a complete standstill: the Cid does not, and has made no plans to, share his political power with his sons-in-law. Hence, the infantes must petition the Cid to allow them to return to their beloved Carrión. Given these conditions, the Cid could not possibly deny there petition. Consequently, the introduction of the episode that gives rise to lines 2532–34 and lines 2535–36 constitutes a parelcon, a superfluous addition that serves no morphologic-structural purpose. As a matter of fact, the narrator himself will shortly prove this to be the case. And with this final observation, Move 5 can now commence. The symbolic transcription of Move 5 is as follows:

$$\underline{a}BCDF\uparrow K^4$$
$$\{a\}$$

(The above symbolic transcription corresponds to the numerical functions: VIIIa, IX, X, XII, XIV, XI, and XIX.) Move 5 begins with the infantes longing to return to Carrión: "—Vayamos pora Carrión, aquí mucho detardamos. / Los averes que tenemos grandes son e sobejanos, / mientra que visquiéremos despender no los podremos—" (ll. 2540–42) ["'Let us set off for Carrión; we delay too long here; / the wealth we possess is great and magnificent; / in all our days we cannot spend it all'"]. These lines do not require the aetiologic foundation of derision that the narrator assigns to them: the grounds that I have outlined above justify them. Moreover, don Fernando and don Diego, the manipulated puppets of the omniscient raconteur, promptly deconstruct their narrator's thesis that ridicule constitutes the aetiologic root of their resolve to abandon Valencia. The underlying reason behind this decision lies elsewhere, in their obsessive need to satisfy a present lack. Once they are beyond the reach of the Cid, they will be at liberty to express their deeply harbored resentment against don Rodrigo (resentment that aetiologically rests on the lion episode in Move 3) by vicariously enacting their revenge on their defenseless and innocent wives ({a}):

—Pidamos nuestras mugieres al Cid Campeador,
digamos que las levaremos a tierras de Carrión,
e enseñarlas hemos dó las heredades son.
Sacarlas hemos de Valencia, de poder del
 Campeador;
después en la carrera feremos nuestro sabor,
ante que nos retrayan lo que cuntió del león.
Nós de natura somos de condes de Carrión,
averes levaremos grandes que valen grant valor,
escarniremos las fijas del Canpeador.
 D'aquestos averes sienpre seremos ricos omnes,

   podremos casar con fijas de reyes o de
                enperadores,
   ca de natura somos de condes de Carrión.
   Assí las escarniremos a las fijas del Campeador
   antes que nos retrayan lo que fue del león.—
                (ll. 2543–56)
["Let us ask My Cid the Battler to allow our wives to
              accompany us.
Let us say we are going to take them to the lands of
              Carrión
and to show them where their estates are.
We shall take them away from Valencia, out of the
           power of the Battler,
and then on the journey we shall do all we wish with
               them,
before the business of the lion can be thrown in our
               face;
for we are of the line of the counts of Carrión.
We shall take with us vast riches, possessions great
              of value;
and we shall humiliate the Battler's daughters!
With this wealth we shall for ever be rich men,
and we shall be able to marry the daughters of kings
              or emperors,
for we are of the line of counts of Carrión!
So, we shall humiliate the Battler's daughters,
before the affair of the lion can be thrown in our
               face."]

  What confounds the reader at this juncture is why the poet did not catch himself and backtrack to eliminate the previous palace scene depicting the derision of the vassals of the Cid toward the infantes of Carrión. Once don Fernando and don Diego have obtained their share of the booty taken from the Moors in line 2509, the structure of the diegesis would justify the introduction of the above-quoted passages of lines 2540–42 and lines 2543–56. I should add here, in passing, that there is no justification for the infantes' statement that introduces the motif of unequal social station—namely, that their present economic condition warrants their marrying to the daughters of kings or emperors. It is a gratuitous deus ex machina remark in that the comment has no foundation on narrative passages following the marriages of don Fernando and don Diego to doña Elvira and doña Sol. As far as the reader of the epic poem is concerned, the narrator's original illocutionary comment regarding the affective state of don Fernando and don Diego when they married doña Elvira and doña Sol: "Amos las reciben   d'amor e de grado" (l. 2234) ["They both received them with love and pleasure"], still holds true at the time they plan their return to their estate in Carrión. The narrator's insistence on bringing up the motif of unequal social station in later passages constitutes an aesthetic defect, an error that weakens considerably the otherwise coherent artistic structure of the final sections of the epic poem.

Having made up their minds to avenge themselves on the Cid— their mediate objective ({a})—the infantes must leave Valencia with an excuse that would meet with the approval of the Cid. The infantes' stated desire to return with their wives to their lands in Carrión, from which they have been absent for many years, will serve as the ruse that don Fernando will pitch to the Cid (a). Don Fernando's petition to the Cid and to the members of the Cid's court is pleasant to the ears of his audience, since he endeavors to express himself artistically by extensively employing various rhyme patterns. There is one consonant-oxytone rhyme of "or"; five consonant-paroxytone cases of "emos"; three assonant-paroxytone rhymes of "e-a"; one assonant-paroxytone rhyme of "a-a"; and one assonant-paroxytone rhyme of "a-o""a-o":

    —¡Sí vos vala el Criador,   Cid Campeador!
    Que plega a doña Ximena   e primero a vós,
    e a Minaya Álbar Fáñez   e a cuantos aquí son:
    dadnos nuestras mugieres   que avemos a
                                  bendiciones,
    levarlas hemos   a nuestras tierras de Carrión,
    meterlas hemos   en las villas
    que les diemos   por arras e por onores.
    Verán vuestras fijas   lo que avemos nós,
    los fijos que oviéremos   en qué avrán partición.—
                                  (ll. 2559–67)

["May the Creator protect you, O Cid the Battler!
May what I ask please Doña Jimena, and you before all,
and Minaya Álvar Fáñez and all those here present!
Give us our wives, our marriage to whom has been blessed;
we are going to take them to our lands in Carrión,
and put them in possession of the properties
which we have given them as wedding gifts and as an inheritance.
Your daughters shall see what we possess,
and what it is that our children will share."]

Don Rodrigo has no reason to suspect treason on the part of the infantes or to believe that their request harbors dark, criminal designs: "De assí ser afontado no s' curiava el Campeador" (l. 2569) ["The Cid, who did not suspect that he was to be dishonoured"]. Hence, he immediately grants don Fernando's request, becoming the dispatcher of the infantes (B), who here assume the role of heroes (C). By showering the couples with monetary and nonmonetary gifts, the Cid assumes, as well, the role of donor (DF). Among the gifts, the Cid includes three thousand marks and his two precious swords, Colada and Tizón.

The several scenes of leave-taking that ensue within and without the palace constitute emotional segmental interludes. The Cid bids his children his last adieu (↑) at the outskirts of Valencia, and then returns to his palace. Don Rodrigo's departure liquidates the immediate initial lack of the infantes—that is, their need to leave Valencia and to be free of the Cid (K^4). Move 5 closes with two segmental interludes. The first is a deus ex machina passage, in which the Cid perceives omens that the narrator neither describes nor explains, which presage a calamitous ending to the marital relationship between his daughters and the infantes: "Violo en los avueros   el que en buen ora cinxo espada / que estos casamientos   non serién sin alguna tacha; / no s' puede repentir,   que casadas las ha amas" (ll. 2615–17) ["But the man who girded his sword in a favoured hour saw from the omens / that these marriages would not be without some stain; / he could not repent now, for he had married them both"]. The second segmental interlude passage relates to the Cid's decision to send Félix

Muñoz, his nephew, to accompany the infantes' entourage to ensure that his daughters arrive safely in Carrión.

Move 6 (Cantar III)
In Move 6, the narrator renders the infantes' encounter with the Moor Abengalbón, a friend of the Cid. Below is the symbolic transcription of Move 6:

$$aC{\uparrow}D{:}F{:}^{1,\,9}G^2E^9\text{var}.\S H\text{-}I\text{-}K^4\text{-}$$

(The above symbolic transcription corresponds to the numerical functions: VIIIa, X, XI, XII, XIV, XV, XIII, XVI, XVIII, and XIX.)

Move 6 commences with the infantes and their entourage setting off to Carrión without an escort (a). They spend a night in Albarracín, and then, in a passage that marks a foreshortening of space and time, they arrive at Molina ($C\uparrow$). There the Moor Abengalbón, upon the request of the Cid's emissary Félix Muñoz, meets up with them and takes on the role of donor. He addresses their every need, and he puts himself at the disposal of the infantes and their wives (DF). He and his company of two hundred horsemen escort the party to Ansarera (G^2), where he showers doña Elvira and doña Sol with additional unspecified gifts and presents the infantes with two horses ($DF^{1,9}$). Impressed with Abengalbón's affluence, the infantes, who regard Abengalbón now as their enemy, converse among themselves about the advantages of assassinating the Moor and stealing his wealth (E^9 var.: the reaction of the hero to the actions of the donor):

—Ya pues que a dexar avemos   fijas del
                                                  Campeador,
si pudiéssemos matar   el moro Avengalvón,
cuanta riquiza tiene   averla iemos nós,
tan en salvo lo abremos   commo lo de Carrión,
nuncua avrié derecho de nós   el Cid Campeador.—
                                              " (ll. 2661–65)
["Now, since we are going to abandon the Battler's
                                              daughters,
if we could kill the Moor Abengalbón,
we would take all his wealth.

> It would be as securely ours as our possessions in
> Carrión,
> and My Cid the Battler would have no claim on us."]

A Moor, with an understanding of Spanish, coincidently overhears the latter conversation and relates it immediately to Abengalbón. The Moor's communication constitutes a connective link (§) to the function that immediately follows. Abengalbón and his two hundred armed horsemen, in turn, gallop to where the infantes are resting and, once in the camp of the infantes, the Moor confronts the two brothers. Abengalbón opens his discourse with a hypophora and continues with an onedismus and categoria—that is, he immediately answers his own question and reproaches them as ungrateful and berates them for their wickedness. Then he abandons them to the whims and wiles of Dame Fortune, refusing to be of any further service to them:

> —Dezidme, ¿qué vos fiz, ifantes?
> Yo sirviéndovos sin art e vós, pora mí, muert
> consejastes.
> Si no lo dexás por mio Cid el de Bivar,
> tal cosa vos faría que por el mundo sonás,
> e luego levaría sus fijas al Campeador leal.
> ¡Vós nuncua en Carrión entrariedes jamás!
> Aquí m' parto de vós commo de malos e de
> traidores.— (ll. 2675–81)
> ["Tell me what I have done to you, Infantes of
> Carrión.
> Though I served you without malice, you plotted my
> death.
> Were I not to hold back on account of My Cid of
> Vivar,
> I would do such a thing to you that news of it
> would echo throughout the world,
> and then I would take back to the loyal Battler his
> daughters.
> You would never re-enter Carrión!

> Here and now I take my leave of you as evil and treacherous men."]

For the infantes the result is failure. They failed to confront their enemy, and instead he confronted them; they were not victorious over their enemy, but their enemy defeated them (H-I-). Lastly, the original lack of an escort remains unresolved at the end of Move 6 (K^4-).[8]

As for the function of Move 6, the diegesis relating the infantes' encounter with the Moor Abengalbón serves to underscore the fact that unbridled greed still remains the ingrained psychological trait of the infantes and that it determines and drives the daily pragmatic conduct of both don Fernando and don Diego. Along with their insatiable passion to acquire material wealth, the narrator has added another element to their unattractive, despicable characters, namely, that of villainy. To satisfy further their continuous craving for wealth, the infantes are even willing to commit murder. This violent and undisclosed character flaw of don Fernando and don Diego prepares the reader for what is to transpire next in Move 7 of this diegesis of the infantes of Carrión.

Move 7 (Cantar III)

In Move 7 the narrator details the infantes' flogging and abandonment of the daughters of the Cid at Corpes. The symbolic transcription of Move 7 appears below:

$$a^6 BCMN\{K^4\} \downarrow$$

(The above symbolic transcription corresponds to the numerical functions: {VIII}, VIIIa, IX, X, XXV, XXVI, {XIX}, and XX.)

This brief move commences with an extensive segmental interlude passage. Following the browbeating session from the Moor Abengalbón, the infantes and their entourage leave Ansarera. Traveling "de día e de noch" (l. 2690) ["by day and by night"], they traverse in four lines (another case of spatial and temporal foreshortening) the mountains of Miedes, the Montes Claros, and the villages of Griza and San Esteban (ll. 2692–94 and l. 2696). In Corpes, wherein, as the narrator informs his reader, roam "bestias fieras" (l. 2699) ["wild beasts"], a reference that constitutes an ineffective artistic expression since the narrator never presents a situation that justifies his illocutionary statement. Here, they pitch their tents and spend the night making love to their wives. Anticipating the act of revenge that is to ensue the next day, the narrator issues the following proleptic ecphonesis: "'¡mal ge lo cunplieron   cuando salié el sol!" (l. 2704) ["But how ill they kept their vows when the sun rose!"]. In the morning don Fernando and don Diego order those in their entourage to continue on their journey to Carrión while they remain behind with their wives, according to the narrator, to make merry: "deportarse quieren con ellas   a todo su sabor" (l. 2711) ["they wanted to enjoy themselves with them at their pleasure"]. However, this stated reason is a ruse: their real intent is to carry out their revenge vicariously on the Cid through his daughters, doña Elvira and doña Sol. Alone with their wives, the infantes inform them of their intention to get revenge on don Rodrigo for the lion incident by flogging them first and, then, abandoning them in Corpes (a[6]):

—Bien lo creades,   don Elvira e doña Sol,
aquí seredes escarnidas,   en estos fieros montes,
oy nos partiremos   e dexadas seredes de nós,
non abredes part   en tierras de Carrión.
Irán aquestos mandados   al Cid Campeador,
nós vengaremos   por aquésta la del león.—
(ll. 2714–19)
["You can well believe, Doña Elvira and Doña Sol,
that you will be thoroughly humiliated in this wild
forest.
Today we shall part, and you will be abandoned by
us;
you will have no share in the lands of Carrión.
News of this will go to the Cid the Battler;
this will be our revenge for being humiliated with the
lion"]

Again, the illocutionary reference to "fieros montes" constitutes another ineffective artistic expression even though it is an utterance made by one of the infantes. The lines that follow never corroborate the existence of "bestias fieras" in the mountainous woods of Corpes. Nevertheless, the remark about "fieros montes" does constitute a bitingly ironic phrase in that in these "fieros montes" the only "fierce beasts" to be found on these grounds will turn out to be Fernando González and Diego González, the infantes of Carrión. Savagely, Don Fernando and don Diego proceed to strip their wives of their clothing, allowing for only silk gowns to cover their bodies. After entreating their husband in vain that they behead them instead of flogging them, Doña Elvira and doña Sol pronounce the following admonition that will prove to be prophetic (B): "—Atán malos ensiemplos non fagades sobre nós; / si nós fuéremos majadas, abiltaredes a vós, / retraérvoslo han en vistas o en cortes—" (ll. 2731–33) ["'Do not make such wretched examples of us! / If we are beaten, you will bring dishonour on yourselves, / and you will be accountable for it at an assembly or at a royal court'"]. The infantes dismiss their wives' admonitory words and immediately commence to batter doña Elvira and doña Sol with their cinches and spurs (C):

> Lo que ruegan las dueñas non les ha ningún pro,
> essora les conpieçan a dar los ifantes de Carrión,
> con las cinchas corredizas májanlas tan sin sabor;
> con las espuelas agudas, don ellas an mal sabor,
> ronpién las camisas e las carnes a ellas amas a dós.
> Linpia salié la sangre sobre los ciclatones,
> ya lo sienten ellas en los sos coraçones.
> (ll. 2734–40)
> [The ladies' plea is in vain.
> Now the Infantes of Carrión begin to beat them.
> With the saddle-girths they strike them cruelly,
> and with their sharp spurs they cut into them to cause them great pain,
> tearing through the undergarments of each of them and into their flesh.
> Brightly their blood flows out onto the silk.
> They feel such pain in their hearts!]

In the above passage the narrator accentuates the pragmatographia of the relentless beating of doña Elvira and doña Sol by using the verb "ronpién," which denotes destruction by separation, detachment, and laceration, as a prozeugma at the beginning of line 2738. Following this verb are two nouns that, given the alliteration of the consonant sounds "k" and "s," fix the reader's eye first on the words "camisas" / "carnes" (l. 2738) and later on the noun "sangre;" the latter is underscored, in turn, by the alliteration of the consonant "s" in "salié" / "sangre" / "sobre" (l. 2739) and the assonant-paroxytone rhyme "a-e" of "carnes" / "sangre" (ll. 2738–39). As for the flow of blood emerging from the wounds of these two women, the narrator emphasizes it by repeating the liquid consonant "l" throughout the following lines: "ronpién las camisas e las carnes a ellas amas a dós. / Linpia salié la sangre sobre los ciclatones" (ll. 2738–39). At this point, the narrator decides to cut into his diegesis and insert a personal ecphonesis-optatio that is, at the same time, an apostrophe and an abbreviated deesis or appeal: "¡Cuál ventura serié ésta, sí ploguiesse al Criador, / que assomasse essora el Cid Campeador!" (ll. 2741-42) ["What a blessing it would be if it were to please the Creator / that at this moment the Cid the Battler should appear!"]. (A shortened version of the latter appears ten lines below: "¡Cuál ventura serié si assomás essora el Cid Campeador!" [l. 2753] [What a blessing it would be if the Cid the Battler were to appear now!"].) This narratorial segmental interlude is, indeed, ironic. It is ironic—my commentary applies to line 2753, as well—for two reasons. On the one hand, the narrator is omniscient and, thereby, knows where all his characters are at any given moment. As a result, he is most definitely aware that neither God nor he can extract the Cid from Valencia and magically fly him into Corpes except by a deus ex machina improvisation. On the other hand, he knows very well that, if he so wished, he could place his created character Félix Muñoz, the nephew of the Cid who has accompanied the Cid's daughters thus far in their journey to Carrión, close to this occurrence so that he may rescue them and initiate their return to Valencia. The latter, in fact, is what the narrator does. Hence, the omniscient narrator's emotional intrusion in the text fails to provide greater pathos to the scene; instead, it brings with it a pause whose melodramatic tone constitutes an unaesthetic distraction.

To return to the narrative: The infantes' unceasing battering of their wives leaves them exhausted: "Cansados son de ferir ellos amos a dos" (l.2745)["Both men have grown tired with beating them"], and their wives, doña Elvira and doña Sol, unconscious: "Tanto las majaron que sin cosimente son" (l. 2743) ["They beat them until they are numb"].[9, 10] Abandoning their wives for dead in the forest, don Fernando and don Diego depart to rejoin their entourage, boasting of having fulfilled the difficult task they had set out to accomplish (MN$\{K^4\}\downarrow$):

> Por los montes do ivan, ellos ívanse alabando:
> —De nuestros casamientos agora somos
>   vengados,
> non las deviemos tomar por varraganas si non
>   fuéssemos rogados,
> pues nuestras parejas non eran pora en braços.
> ¡La desondra del león assí s'irá vengando!—
>   (ll. 2757–62)
> [As they rode through the forest, the Infantes boasted
>   to each other:
> "Now we have our revenge for our marriages.
> We ought not to have accepted them even as
>   concubines,
> had we not been formally requested to do so.
> They were not our equals in status, to be our wives.
> In this way the dishonour brought on us by the lion
>   will be avenged."]

To bring down the curtain on Move 7, I should like to point out several things regarding the infantes' discourse. First, they ascribe to others and not to themselves their marriages to the daughters of don Rodrigo—the latter constitutes an interesting psychological act of displacement. Second, they make reference once more to the motif of unequal social station that exists between them and their wives—words that serve to erase in the minds of don Fernando and don Diego all feelings of guilt and sin associated with their barbarous actionl against doña Elvira and doña Sol. (In passing, the above two statements constitute instances of dramatic irony, since the reader of the *Cantar de Mio Cid* knows that both statements are false.) Third, the infantes' remarks raise a grave moral question. They bring to the fore the claim regarding the principle of aristocratic social privilege—namely, that the canons of morality and justice that govern the everyday state of affairs of the underprivileged, ordinary, classless masses do not apply to those of aristocratic rank.

Move 8 (Cantar III)

Move 8 deals with the trial of don Fernando and don Diego in the court that King Alfonso holds in Toledo and the subsequent duels they must engage in with Pedro Bermúdez and Martín Antolínez in Carrión. The symbolic transcription of Move 8 follows:

$$A^8 B{:}^4 \; \underline{C}\text{-} \; \{\uparrow G^2\} L \vdots M{:}\underline{N}{:}$$
$$\phantom{A^8 B{:}^4 \;\;} C \phantom{\text{-} \; \{\uparrow G^2\} L \vdots M{:}} N\text{-}$$

(The above symbolic transcription corresponds to the numerical functions: VIII, IX, X, {XI, XV}, XXIV, XXV, and XXVI.)

Move 8 results from a single complaint that Muño Gustioz, the Cid's emissary, raises in the presence of King Alfonso in Sahagún. On the basis of the infantes' flogging and abandonment of the daughters of the Cid at Corpes—an occurrence that, while affecting the honor of don Rodrigo, pertains specifically to the honor of the king for his having married the Cid's daughters to the infantes of Carrión—Muño Gustioz requests that the monarch hold a special judicial meeting to try don Fernando and don Diego. Since the Cid is the enemy of the infantes, any complaint don Rodrigo raises that is pertinent to the infantes must constitute, perforce, a villainous act. Hence, Muño Gustioz's grievance amounts to that of a villain making a false demand (A^8).

King Alfonso accedes to the above petition and sends heralds to inform the nobles of his realm that he will hold court in Toledo within seven weeks to resolve the Cid's grievance against the two brothers of Carrión, underscoring that if they fail to attend, they will forfeit their standing as his vassals (B^4). The infantes accede to his orders only after King Alfonso threatens to exile them from his realm if they do not appear (C). From a psychological point of view, the passage that follows underscores the unconscious feeling of guilt that don Fernando and don Diego have regarding their actions at Corpes: "miedo han que ý verná mio Cid el Campeador" (l. 2987) ["they were afraid that My Cid the Battler would be there"]. Artistically, the passage contains several interior rhyme cases. There are four assonant-paroxytone rhymes, that of "e-e" (l. 2988 and ll. 2992–93), "e-a" (l. 2989), and "e-o" (ll. 2987–88) and one consonant-paroxytone rhyme, that of "edo" (ll. 2986–87):

> Ya les va pesando   a los ifantes de Carrión
> porque el rey   en Toledo fazié cort,
> miedo han que ý verná   mio Cid el Campeador.
> Prenden so consejo   assí parientes commo son,
> ruegan al rey   que los quite d'esta cort;
> dixo el rey: —No lo feré,   sí n' salve Dios,
> ca ý verná   mio Cid el Campeador,
> darl'edes derecho,   ca rencura ha de vós.
> Qui lo fer non quisiesse   o no ir a mi cort
> quite mio reino,   ca d'el non he sabor.—
> (ll. 2985–94)
> [Now the Infantes of Carrión were saddened,
> because, in Toledo, the King was holding his court.
> They were afraid that My Cid the Battler would be there.
> They sought the advice of all their relatives,
> and asked the King to exempt them from attendance at the court.
> The King said: "I shall not, may God save me!
> For My Cid the Battler will be there,
> and you are to give him justice as he has a grievance against you.
> Anyone who is unwilling to obey or who fails to attend my court
> is to leave my kingdom, for he will not enjoy my favor."]

The infantes arrive at the court in Toledo on the day designated by King Alfonso—the functions of dekparture and spatial transference between kingdoms are tacit: ($\{\uparrow G^2\}$)—; the Cid, in turn, arrives five days later. At the court, don Rodrigo establishes, quite astutely, that the brutal beating and abandonment of doña Elvira and doña Sol constitute an issue of honor that concerns the king, and he proceeds to formulate his grievances against the infantes. From the point of view of don Fernando and don Diego, the Cid's three grievances constitute unfounded claims (L).

Of the three—another instance of the folkloric phenomenon of trebling—two relate to material matters. All the complaints, in turn, set up difficult tasks for the infantes (M), even though only the first two directly concern the person of the Cid. The brothers of Carrión can either comply with the demands the Cid makes of them (N) or not (N).

In his first charge, don Rodrigo demands that the infantes return to him his swords, Colada and Tizón, since they had accepted those items in bad faith (M). In this passage, the Cid employs two assonant-paroxytone rhymes of "a-a" (ll. 3152–53 and ll. 3157–58) to highlight just how important the issue of the swords is to him. Don Rodrigo's final expressed demand closes his discursive enthymeme with a hammer-like blow—underscored by the consonant-paroxytone rhyme "ieron" (l. 3157), the assonant-paroxytone rhyme "e-o" (ll. 3157–58), and the assonant-paroxytone rhyme "a-a" (ll. 3157–58)—directed at the heads of the two brothers of Carrión:

> —Mas cuando sacaron mis fijas   de Valencia la mayor,
> yo bien los quería   d'alma e de coraçón,
> diles dos espadas,   a Colada e a Tizón
> (éstas las gané   a guisa de varón),
> que s'ondrassen con ellas   e sirviessen a vós.
> Cuando dexaron mis fijas   en el robredo de Corpes,
> conmigo non quisieron aver nada   e perdieron mi amor:
> ¡denme mis espadas   cuando mios yernos non son!— (ll. 3151–58)
> ["But when from the great city of Valencia they took my daughters,
> whom I love tenderly, with my heart and soul,
> I gave them two swords, Colada and Tizón,
> which I had won in manly combat,
> that with them they might win honour and serve you.
> When they abandoned my daughters in the oak-wood at Corpes,
> they wanted to have nothing to do with me, and forfeited my love.

> Let them give me back my swords, since they are no longer my sons-in-law."]

Thankful that the Cid has not charged them with the beating of his two daughters, don Fernando and don Diego are confident that they can reach a reasonable settlement with King Alfonso were he, subsequently, to raise the question of honor with them. Thus the infantes decide to return the two swords to don Rodrigo. The infantes are convinced that doing so constitutes the sole claim that don Rodrigo has against them and that by thus complying with the judges' finding in favor of the Battler they will rid themselves forevermore of the Cid:

> —Aún grand amor nos faze el Cid Campeador
> cuando desondra de sus fijas no nos demanda oy,
> bien nos avendremos con el rey don Alfonso.
> Démosle sus espadas, cuando assí finca la boz,
> e cuando las toviere partirse á la cort,
> ya más non avrá derecho de nós el Cid
> Canpeador.— (ll. 3164–69)
> ["The Cid the Battler indeed shows us great favor
> in not calling us to reckoning today for his daughters' dishonour;
> we shall indeed come to an agreement with King Alfonso.
> Let us give him his swords since he rests his case at this,
> and when he has them he must leave the court;
> the Cid the Battler will no longer have a claim on us."]

Handing over the two swords to King Alfonso, don Fernando and don Diego comply with the Cid's demand (N).

Unfortunately, the infantes have erred in thinking that their conflict with the Cid stopped there. The Cid brings forth a second complaint against the infantes, creating a second difficult task for them. He demands that they return to him the sum of three thousand marks he gave them as part of his daughters' dowry (M):

—Otra rencura he de ifantes de Carrión,
cuando sacaron de Valencia mis fijas amas a dos,
en oro e en plata tres mill marcos les di yo;
yo faziendo esto, ellos acabaron lo so:
¡denme mis averes, cuando mios yernos non
son!— (ll. 3202–6)
["I have another grievance against the Infantes of
Carrión:
when they took my two daughters away from
Valencia,
in gold and silver I gave them three thousand marks.
In spite of this, they carried out their plan;
let them return my money, since they are no longer
my sons-in-law."]

    The infantes' counterclaim that the Cid has no right to make such a demand: "—Por esso˙l' diemos sus espadas al Cid Campeador, / que ál no nos demandasse, que aquí fincó la boz—" (ll. 3210–11) ["'We returned the swords to the Cid the Battler / that he should ask no more of us; there he rested his case'"]. This counterclaim receives no support among the judges of their noble peers. Inexplicably, don Fernando and don Diego have managed to spend most of the funds they were given. This situation constitutes a deus ex machina occurrence, since nothing stated in the text warrants such a state of affairs. Consequently, the infantes are unable to comply with this demand to repay in silver and gold the monies for which they are beholden to don Rodrigo. The brothers of Carrión state that they will deed over property from their estate in Carrión to the Cid in lieu of the monies they owe him: "—Pagarle hemos de heredades en tierras de Carrión—" (l. 3223) ["'We shall pay him in property from our estates at Carrión'"]. Their proposal does not meet with the approval of the judges at the court, and they oblige the infantes to repay the sum of three thousand marks in the form of goods such as swords and horses that they and their retinue have brought with them to the court (N).
    The third complaint the Cid voices against the infantes is in regard to their comportment against his daughters at Corpes. Don Rodrigo finds their behavior unjustified and publicly refers to them metaphorically as

"canes traidores" (l. 3263) ["treacherous dogs"] before King Alfonso and the other nobles present in the court. Don Fernando and don Diego, given that they consider their action at Corpes meritorious, view the Cid's reproof of their moral character negatively (L). (Note that the words of the Cid constitute a personal ethical-moral evaluation of their respective characters and, as such, do not give rise to any difficult task for the infantes to perform. Don Fernando and don Diego have nothing to give back to the Cid to assuage his last grievance.) The infantes, and those that sympathize with the cause of don Fernando and don Diego, rebuke the Cid's judgment, invoking the prerogative of superior social station. Count don García avers that the relatively low social station of doña Elvira and doña Sol do not make them worthy of being the concubines of don Fernando and don Diego, let alone their wives: "—non ge las devién querer   sus fijas por varraganas / o ¿quién ge las diera   por parejas o por veladas?—" (ll. 3276–77) ["'that they ought not to want his daughters even as concubines. / Who then gave them as partners in marriage?'"]. Don Fernando follows suit in the same vein:

>—De natura somos   de condes de Carrión,
>deviemos casar con fijas   de reyes o de
>   enperadores,
>ca non pertenecién   fijas de ifançones;
>porque las dexamos   derecho fiziemos nós,
>más nos preciamos,   sabet, que menos no.—
>   (ll. 3296–300)
>["We are of the line of the counts of Carrión!
>We should have married daughters of kings or
>   emperors,
>for the daughters of lesser nobles were not suitable
>   for us,
>We were right to abandon them.
>We consider ourselves the more honoured, I tell you,
>   not less."]

The fact that don Rodrigo must refrain from exacting satisfaction from the infantes of Carrión for having flogged and abandoned his daughters does not mean that his vassals, in turn, must do so as well. At the urging of the Cid, Pedro Bermúdez speaks up and, denouncing don Fernando as a coward (his reference is to the latter's fleeing from a Moor at the start of the past battle against King Búcar), he challenges don Fernando to a duel. In turn, don Diego, claiming privilege of superior social station, boasts about what they did to the Cid's daughters at Corpes and declares his willingness to duel with anyone over this matter:

> —De natura somos   de los condes más linpios,
> estos casamientos   non fuessen aparecidos,
> por consagrar   con mio Cid don Rodrigo.
> Porque dexamos sus fijas   aún no nos repentimos;
> mientra que bivan   pueden aver sospiros,
> lo que les fiziemos   serles ha retraído.
> ¡Esto lidiaré   a tod el más ardido:
> que porque las dexamos   ondrados somos nós!—
>   (ll. 3354–60)
> ["By nature we are counts of the purest descent!
> I wish that these marriages had never taken place,
> that we should be related by blood to My Cid Don
>   Rodrigo!
> We have not repented of abandoning his daughters.
> As long as they live they can continue to sigh,
> and they will be taunted with what we did to them.
> Over this, I will fight against the boldest,
> for because we abandoned them we are honoured."]

Replying to the above words of don Diego, Martín Antolínez states that he accepts his challenge to a duel. Lastly, Muño Gustioz challenges Asur González to a duel after the latter demeans the aristocratic standing of the Cid: "—Fuesse a río d'Ovirna   los molinos picar / e prender maquilas, commo lo suele far. / ¿Quí l' darié   con los de Carrión a casar?—" (ll. 3379–81) ["'He should go to the Ubierna river [*sic*] to dress the millstones / and to collect money for the grain as is his custom. / Who could imagine him related by marriage to those of Carrión?'"]. All the above challenges to a duel constitute difficult tasks (M).

      Three weeks later, at Carrión, the duels between these individuals take place and the infantes and Asur González fail to fulfill the difficult task of defeating the Cid's representatives in their respective duels (N-). Their defeat brings closure to Tale 11. The Tale of Fernando González and Diego González, the Infantes of Carrión.

Chapter 5. The Tale of the Revenge of the Cid on the Infantes of Carrión and the Remarriage of Doña Elvira and Doña Sol to the Infante of Navarre and Infante of Aragón

The tale of the revenge of the Cid on the infantes of Carrión constitutes the sixteenth tale of the *Cantar de Mio Cid*. This tale consists of four short moves. The first move focuses on the manner in which the Cid plans to bring his grievances against the don Fernando and don Diego; the second move deals with the Cid's recovery of certain materialistic items he gave to the infantes; and the third and fourth moves entail the erasure of the dishonor that the two brothers of Carrion have inflicted on the Cid and on his daughters in battering doña Elvira and doña Sol in the woods of Corpes. The results of the fourth move, in turn, permit the Cid, who has regained his honor, to remarry immediately his two daughters to the infantes of Aragón and Navarre, two noblemen related to King Alfonso.

Move 1 (Cantar III)
In this move the Cid convinces King Alfonso to hold a special court to try the infantes of Carrión. Below is the symbolic transcription of this move:

$$\alpha aBC\uparrow\{G^2\}L\text{-}MN\{\downarrow\}$$

(The above symbolic transcription corresponds to the numerical functions: VIIIa, IX, X, XI, {XV}, XXIV, XXV, XXVI, and {XX}.)

The initial situation of Move 1 finds the daughters of the Cid safely back in Valencia after the ordeal they endured at the hands of their husbands at Corpes (α). The abusive comportment of the infantes shows disrespect to both the daughters and their parents, classifying the Díaz family as belonging to a lower aristocratic class, as if they were almost commoners, to be used and abused at will by those belonging to the old and distinguished Spanish aristocracy. Don Rodrigo must take steps to regain his honor (a), and this he does immediately. He sends Muño Gustioz as his emissary to King Alfonso. Don Rodrigo instructs Muño

Gustioz to communicate to the king that he wishes to bring the infantes of Carrión to trial to repossess material objects, although at this point the Cid does not identify the specific items in question (B): "—Mios averes se me han levado   que sobejanos son, / esso me puede pesar   con la otra desonor—" (ll. 2912–13) ["'They have carried off possessions of mine, which are very great, / and that can cause me sorrow, together with the other dishonour'"]. The reference to "la otra desonor" alludes to the infantes' ignominious and barbaric comportment inflicted upon his daughters at Corpes. Even though don Rodrigo is primarily concerned with the abusive actions of the infantes, which have brought shame and dishonor to his family's name, he is very careful to emphasize to Muño Gustioz that he abrogates his right to seek satisfaction from don Fernando and don Diego on this score because their behavior primarily reflects upon King Alfonso. By their deliberate act of savagery perpetrated against doña Elvira and doña Sol at Corpes, the infantes have insulted and dishonored the king, for it was he who had commanded don Rodrigo to marry his two daughters to the infantes of Carrión:

—D'esta desondra que me an fecha   los ifantes de
                                                        Carrión
que l' pese al buen rey   d'alma e de coraçón.
Él casó mis fijas,   ca non ge las dí yo;
cuando las han dexadas   a grant desonor,
si desondra ý cabe   alguna contra nós,
la poca e la grant   toda es de mio señor.—
                                                        (ll. 2906–11)
["At this dishonour done to me by the Infantes of
                                                        Carrión
let the good King in heart and soul be saddened.
He married my daughters to the Infantes, not I.
Since they have abandoned them, in great dishonour,
if in this there is any affront to my honour,
whether small or great, it is entirely the concern of my
                                                        lord."]

Muño Gustioz accepts the contract to represent the Cid before the king (C) and departs (↑) to visit with King Alfonso. Immediately thereafter

Muño Gustioz stands in front of the king, whom he finds in Sahagún—here spatial and temporal foreshortening renders the function of spatial transference between geographical locations tacit {G^2}. After Muño Gustioz dutifully renders the Cid's pledge of constant obeisance to the king, he delivers his complaint to don Alfonso. Interestingly, of the two complaints that the Cid had voiced to him, Muño Gustioz, by an act of proairesis, disregards the Cid's materialistic grievances and chooses, instead, to communicate to the monarch the single issue regarding the Cid's deliberate forfeiture of his right to obtain retribution. Muño Gustioz bluntly states that the infantes of Carrión have brought dishonor to the Cid, but that his dishonor did not compare to that which the infantes had inflicted upon King Alfonso: "—Tiénes' por desondrado,   mas la vuestra es mayor—" (l. 2950) ["'He <the Cid> considers himself dishonoured, but your dishonour is greater'"]. Muño Gustioz's petition that don Fernando and don Diego be brought to justice echoes the words that doña Elvira and doña Sol stated to their husbands at Corpes. Stylistically, Muño Gustioz's petition is of interest. It contains the figures prozeugma, alloiosis, and tricolon: "—que ge los levedes a vistas   o a juntas o a cortes—" (l. 2949) {"'that you bring them before council or an assembly or at a royal court'"}. His words establish a difficult task for King Alfonso, for the king must decide whether to accept the Cid's claim of having a "derecho" (l. 2952) {"a just cause"} to air publicly his complaints against the two brothers of Carrión (L-M). Acceding to Muño Gustioz's and don Rodrigo's petition, the monarch sends heralds to inform the nobles of his realm that he will hold court in Toledo in seven weeks to resolve the problem raised by the Cid, with the warning that any nobleman not attending this event will forfeit his standing as his royal vassal (N). Once Muño Gustioz has accomplished the mission assigned to him by the Cid, the reader must tacitly assume that the messenger returns to Valencia to rehearse with the Cid the events that had transpired in Sahagún {↓}.

Move 2 (Cantar III)

In Move 2 the Cid recuperates material and equivalent valuables that equal the monies he gave to the infantes of Carrión prior to their departure from Valencia. Following is the symbolic transcription of Move 2:

§a:B:C:L:-M:N:
(The above symbolic transcription corresponds to the numerical functions: VIIIa, IX, X, XXIV, XXV, and XXVI.) Don Rodrigo attends the court of King Alfonso intent on reclaiming certain items he gave to don Fernando and don Diego when they left Valencia with the Cid's daughters to return to Carrión. He arrives five days after the stipulated time the monarch had designated. The meeting with the king, who leaves Toledo to greet the Cid, and don Rodrigo's preparations the following morning to join the other nobles at the Court in Toledo (in lines 3019–3106) constitute parenthetical fill-in incidents. At court, King Alfonso commences Move 2 with an introductory-connective segment in which he announces to the nobles present that he has gathered them to right the wrong committed by the infantes of Carrión against the Cid—the charge of misconduct on the part of don Fernando and don Diego against don Rodrigo constitutes an indisputable fact: "Grande tuerto le han tenido, sabémoslo todos nós" (l. 3134) ["They have done him great wrong, we all know"]; he assigns a number of nobles to serve as judges in this case against the brothers of Carrión; and he yields to don Rodrigo so that he may announce to the nobles at the court his grievances and / or items he wishes to recover from Don Fernando and don Diego, the infantes of Carrión (§).

Addressing King Alfonso and his audience of noble peers, don Rodrigo immediately proceeds to announce (which constitutes an astute move on his part) that he abrogates any claim of obtaining satisfaction from the infantes regarding their having battered and abandoned doña Elvira and doña Sol at Corpes. Their actions, the Cid proclaims, has dishonored the king, and it is King Alfonso who must resolve this issue to his satisfaction: "—por mis fijas que m' dexaron   yo non he desonor, / ca vós las casastes, rey,   sabredes qué fer oy—" (ll. 3149–50) ["'I have not been dishonoured because they abandoned my daughters, / for you married them, my king, and you will know what to do today'"]. At this juncture, the grievance of the Cid refers to the lack of his two swords, Colada and Tizón, items that don Rodrigo treasures most among his material possessions (a). Don Rodrigo declares that it was out of his love for don Fernando and don Diego that he had decided to give them the two weapons, the hard-earned trophies he had obtained as booty from his previous battles. Here don Rodrigo assimilates function B: mediation, the connective incident, with function C: beginning counteraction. In short, the Cid maintains that he had given these two swords to the infantes in good faith. Since the brothers of Carrión had accepted these swords under false pretenses—having preplanned the assassination of doña Elvira and doña Sol—the Cid, raising his voice for emphasis, demands in the imperative mood that don Fernando and don Diego return the swords to him (L-): "—¡denme mis espadas   cuando mios yernos non son!—" (l. 3158) ["Let them give me back my swords, since they are no longer my sons-in-law"]. The judges, finding his demand just, adjudicate in the Cid's favor. Don Rodrigo's demand and the judges' adjudication create a difficult task for don Fernando and don Diego (M): they must choose either to comply or to not comply with the judges' decision regarding the Cid's charge. After deliberating with their relatives, don Fernando and don Diego decide to comply with the decision of the judges and they return Colada and Tizón to King Alfonso, who in turn hands the swords over to the Cid (N). The scene in which don Rodrigo gives Colada and Tizón to Pedro Bermúdez and Martín Antolínez, respectively, constitutes a parenthetical incident.

To the chagrin of don Fernando and don Diego, the Cid raises another charge against them. He demands that the infantes reimburse him the three thousand marks (aBCL-) he gave them as a dowry for his daughters: "—¡denme mis averes,   cuando mios yernos non son!—" (l. 3206) ["let them return my money, since they are no longer my sons-in-law"]. The judges unanimously and summarily dismiss the infantes' response that the Cid has no right to make such a claim and, again, the judges side with don Rodrigo. The infantes have inexplicably spent the monies, so they panic because they seem unable to resolve this difficult task (M). The judges reject the infantes' offer that the Cid accept real estate in Carrión in lieu of the monies owed and oblige don Fernando and don Diego to make good on the sum due to don Rodrigo with valuables that they brought with them to the court (N).

Move 3 (Cantar III)
Move 3 commences the process by which the Cid will recuperate not only his daughters' lost honor but his own honor as well. Following is the symbolic transcription of Move 3:

a§BCL̲::M ⋮ Q↓
L::-

(The above symbolic transcription corresponds to the numerical functions: VIIIa, IX, X, XXIV, XXV, and XXVII.) Once don Rodrigo has recovered from the infantes all his past material assets, he proceeds to air his "rencura mayor" {"greatest grievance"} against don Fernando and don Diego, a grievance so grave that "—non se me puede olbidar—" (l. 3254) {"'I cannot forget'"}. This grievance holds no material consequences—that is, he will gain nothing from an economic point of view by declaring it. Don Rodrigo's grievance this time falls within the province of morality and ethics. Moreover, it is a grievance that he has proairetically—that is, by deliberate choice—abrogated regarding any satisfaction, so that whatever he may say at this juncture will bear no immediate consequences. The grievance in question has to do with the supposed dishonor that don Fernando and don Diego have brought upon the Cid's daughters and on his family's name. Hence, what don Rodrigo and his daughters lack is their honor (a). What will follow, and the Cid knows this only too well, is an oral exchange of opinions, an intellectual one at best, regarding the topic of whether the infantes committed an immoral infraction in maltreating their wives.

With the knowledge that he gains nothing except possibly a clear conscience, the Cid takes aim at don Fernando and don Diego indirectly. Instead of delivering illocutionary declarative statements, he prefers to express his views rhetorically with a series of queries that constitute an indirect presentation of legitimate complaints (L-). He begins his discourse with a connective passage (§) that constitutes a perlocutionary utterance, which unfolds as an exuscitatio, an emotional appeal intended to move those in the court to share the same emotions he feels. Given that he is indignant, his appeal to the nobles constitutes, also, a cohortatio and an indignatio. That is, don Rodrigo will attempt to raise his audience to the same level of indignation that pervades every corner of his brain and soul: "—La rencura mayor   non se me puede olbidar; / oídme toda la cort   e pésevos de mio mal—" (ll. 3254–55) ["'I cannot ignore the greatest part of my grievance. / Let all the court hear me, and feel sorrow at my misfortune!'"]. Clearly, don Rodrigo's stand has now radically shifted.

Whereas before he had claimed that the infantes had not dishonored him: "— por mis fijas que m' dexaron yo non he desonor—" (l. 3149) ["'I have not been dishonoured because they abandoned my daughters'"], presently he confesses that they have: "—los ifantes de Carrión, que m' desondraron tan mal, / a menos de riebtos no los puedo dexar—" (ll. 3256–57) ["'The Infantes of Carrión, who inflicted such dishonour upon me, / cannot be allowed by me to escape unchallenged"].

With these words, don Rodrigo, assimilating function B (mediation, the connective incident) with function C (beginning counteraction), embarks on a series of queries that are anacoenoses—that is, he solicits an answer from the infantes. However, the questions he raises constitute examples of onedismus, epiplexis, and categoria in that he reproaches his adversaries and frames his interlocutors as ungrateful and evil individuals. Don Rodrigo interlaces his illocutionary as well as perlocutionary discourse with other figures and tropes such as the following:

anamnesis: (recalling past events);
optatio: "—oídme toda la cort—" (l. 3255) ["'Let all the court hear me'"];
erotesis: "—Dezid, ¿qué vos merecí, ifantes de Carrión, / en juego o en vero o en alguna razón?—" (ll. 3258–59) ["'Tell me: how did I deserve this of you, Infantes, / in jest, or in earnest, or in any respect?'"];
alloiosis: "—¿en juego o en vero o en alguna razón?—" ["in jest, or in earnest, or in any respect?'"];
metaphor: "—¿A qué m' descubriestes las telas del coraçón?—" (l. 3260) ["'Why did you lay bare the very strings of my heart?'"]; "—ya canes traidores—" (l. 3263) ["'you treacherous dogs'"];
bdelygma: "—ya canes traidores—" (l. 3263) ["'you treacherous dogs'"].

Besides the above stylistic factors, don Rodrigo employs numerous rhyme forms to accentuate his grievance. His discourse contains a consonant-oxytone rhyme of "or" (ll. 3253–54), two assonant-paroxytone rhymes of "e-o"(l. 3257, l. 3259), an assonant-oxytone rhyme of the acute "i" (l. 3258), two assonant-paroxytone rhymes of "e-a" (ll. 3260–61, l. 3267), two assonant-paroxytone rhymes of "e-e" (ll. 3262–63, ll. 3268–69), and an assonant-paroxytone rhyme of "a-e" (ll. 3266–67). For its total emotional impact, I cite this passage in its entirety, with allowances made for several of the above-cited lines or phrases that are, perforce, repeated below. I should point out that line 3258 is reminiscent of those words delivered by Abengalbón in his confrontation with the infantes: "—Dezidme,   ¿qué vos fiz, ifantes?—" (l. 2675) ["'Tell me what I have done to you, Infantes of Carrión'"]:

>—¡Merced, ya rey e señor,   por amor de caridad!
>La rencura mayor   non se me puede olbidar;
>oídme toda la cort   e pésevos de mio mal;
>los ifantes de Carrión,   que m' desondraron tan mal,
>a menos de riebtos   no los puedo dexar.
>Dezid, ¿qué vos merecí,   ifantes de Carrión,
>en juego o en vero   o en alguna razón?
>Aquí lo mejoraré   a juvizio de la cort.
>¿A qué m' descubriestes   las telas del coraçón?
>A la salida de Valencia   mis fijas vos di yo
>con muy grand ondra   e averes a nombre.
>Cuando las non queriedes,   ya canes traidores,
>¿por qué las sacávades   de Valencia, sus honores?
>¿A qué las firiestes   a cinchas e a espolones?
>Solas las dexastes   en el robredo de Corpes,
>a las bestias fieras   e a las aves del mont.
>¡Por cuanto les fiziestes,   menos valedes vós!
>Si non recudedes,   véalo esta cort.— (ll. 3253–59,
>   l. 3259*b*, ll. 3260–69)

["I beg a favour, my lord king, for the love of charity! I cannot ignore the greatest part of my grievance. Let all the court hear me, and feel sorrow at my misfortune! The Infantes of Carrión, who inflicted such dishonour upon me, cannot be allowed by me to escape unchallenged. Tell me: how did I deserve this of you, Infantes, in jest, or in earnest, or in any respect? Here, through the judgment of the court, I shall make amends.

Why did you lay bare the very strings of my heart?
On your departure from Valencia, I gave you my daughters,
with great honour and with possessions in abundance.
Since you did not love them, you treacherous dogs,
why did you take them from their lands in Valencia?
For what reasons did you beat them with saddle-girths and spurs?
You left them alone in the oak-wood at Corpes,
prey to the wild beasts and the birds of the forest.
Through what you did you have lost honour!
If you do not give satisfaction, let this court bear witness!"]

Below, I summarize the events of Tale 11 (Move 8) discussed earlier. The first to answer the Cid is Count García, an ally of the González family, who descend from noble and ancient counts from the region of Carrión.[1] Count García defends don Fernando and don Diego on the basis of social superiority, derived from the fact that the ancient, pristine, and noble lineage of the infantes entitles them to the privilege of abusing those who are below them in social station, as in the case of the daughters of the Cid. For him, doña Elvira and doña Sol are not even worthy of being the concubines of the infantes of Carrión, let alone their wives. His answer constitutes a false remark (L). Following a similar line of reasoning as that of Count García, don Fernando and don Diego stand behind their actions taken against doña Elvira and doña Sol at Corpes and, in addition, boast that their actions were meritorious (L).

Since the Cid, for reasons already given above, cannot reply to the infantes, he gets Pedro Bermúdez to defend his female cousins. The tactic that Pedro Bermúdez uses against don Fernando is to rehearse past events, an act of anamnesis on his part, to underscore the cowardly nature of don Fernando. Starting his reply with a categoria, he reproaches don Fernando, accusing him directly of being a liar: "—¡Mientes, Ferrando,   de cuanto dicho has: / por el Campeador   mucho valiestes más!—" (ll. 3313-14) ["'You lie, Fernando, in all you have said! / Through the Battler you gained greatly in prestige.'"]. Next, Pedro Bermúdez states: "—Las tus mañas   yo te las sabré contar—" (l. 3315) ["'I can tell you of how cunning you have been"'] and continues immediately to relate, in a hysteron proteron fashion—that is, in a reverse, temporal order—past occurrences. He recounts what happened during don Fernando's confrontation with a Moor before the battle against King Búcar commenced. He informs the nobles of the court that instead of standing his ground, don Fernando fled from the scene and that it was he, Pedro Bermúdez, who slew the Moor and later allowed don Fernando to claim credit for the event. Next, he informs them that during the loose lion incident in the Cid's palace, don Fernando rushed to hide underneath the bench on which the Cid was taking a nap. Having finished, Pedro Bermúdez challenges don Fernando to a duel.

Martín Antolínez rebukes don Diego from the start and calls him a liar to his face. His words constitute a synecdoche, a categoria, and a bdelygma: "—¡Calla, alevoso, boca sin verdad!—" (l. 3362) ["'Be silent, traitor, mouth without truth!'"]. After this accusation, he proceeds to rehearse how, in the case of the same loose lion incident related above, don Diego fled from the scene to hide and how he then soiled his clothes, clothes that he would never wear again:

—Lo del león non se te deve olvidar:
saliste por la puerta, metístet' al corral,
fústed' meter tras la viga lagar,
más non vestist el manto nin el brial— (ll. 3363
–66)
["You must not forget the episode of the lion:
you fled through the door and hid in the yard,
and kept out of sight behind a beam of the winepress;
you never again put on that cloak and tunic."]

Martín Antolínez finishes his discourse by challenging don Diego to a duel and avers that at the end of the duel don Diego, will confess to being both a liar and a traitor: "—¡Al partir de la lid, por tu boca lo dirás, / que eres traidor e mintist de cuanto dicho has!—" (ll. 3370–71) ["'When you leave the fight, with your own mouth you shall confess / that you are a traitor and have lied in all you said'"].

The last of the infantes' supporters, Asur González, insults the

Cid. His meiosis reduces the Cid to an individual of lower nobility as he tells the Cid that his family had no business becoming legally tied to the infantes of Carrión. Muño Gustioz promptly challenges Asur González to a duel. All duels are cases of a difficult task (M). At this point in the diegesis, King Alfonso calls a halt to the oral sparring between the two groups and sets the time and place of the duels. They are scheduled to take place in three weeks, at Carrión.[2] The following episodes in the court constitute segmental interludes: (1) the arrival of the emissaries of the infante of Navarre and of the infante of Aragón to request that the Cid allow his daughters to marry the latter two infantes; (2) Minaya Álvar Fáñez's paeanismus, his discourse of joy, which stems from the fact that, now, the infantes will have to kiss the hands of doña Elvira and doña Sol since doña Elvira and doña Sol will shortly become queens in their own right; (3) Gómez Peláez's retort to Minaya Álvar Fáñez's above remark; (4) King Alfonso's conversation with the Cid in which he places his person as surety, guaranteeing the safety of the Cid's men who are to participate in the duel in Carrión; and (5) the Cid's magnanimous offer to share with those in the court the material goods he had received from the infantes.

Move 3 ends with King Alfonso recognizing the Cid as a hero (Q): "—¡Yo lo juro   par Sant Esidro el de León / que en todas nuestras tierras   non ha tan buen varón!—" (ll. 3509–10) ["'I swear by Saint Isidore of León / that in all our lands there is no other man so good!'"]. All the parties then take their leave to return to their respective estates ($\downarrow$). Finally, both the Cid's desire to give King Alfonso his horse, Babieca, as a gift and the king's refusal to accept it constitute another segmental interlude.

Move 4 (Cantar III)

In Move 4, the Cid indirectly recuperates his past lost honor and remarries his daughters, doña Elvira and doña Sol, to the infante of Navarre and infante of Aragón.[3] Following is the symbolic transcription of Move 4:

$$a\{C\uparrow G^2\}H : I : \{\downarrow G^2\}K^4W:$$

(The above symbolic transcription corresponds to the numerical functions:

VIIIa, {X, XI, XV}XVI, XVIII, {XX , XV}, XIX, and XXXI.)
Move 4 commences with neither the Cid nor his daughters having recuperated their honor (a). (At this point, the move contains a series of tacit functions involving the Cid's men who travel to Carrión to regain don Rodrigo's and the latter's daughters' honor: their decision upon counteraction {C}, their leaving Toledo {↑}, and their spatial transference between two kingdoms on land {G^2}.) A case of temporal foreshortening follows in which three weeks have transpired from one line to the next:

>Alegre fue d'aquesto   el que en buen ora nació,
>espidiós' de todos   los que sos amigos son,
>mio Cid pora Valencia   e el rey pora Carrión.
>Las tres semanas de plazo   todas complidas son."
>(ll. 3530–33)
>[The man born in a favoured hour was filled with joy at this.
>He took his leave of all those who were his friends.
>My Cid set off for Valencia and the King for Carrión.
>Now the permitted three weeks have passed.]

The following constitute parenthetical interludes: the narrator's revelation to his reader that kinsmen of Carrión brothers had instructions to assassinate the three representatives of the Cid; the narrator's deliberate postponement of the dueling action, which creates suspense by supplying the reader with synchronic passages that describe how both parties prepare for battle; and the narrator's intercalating the negative response of King Alfonso to a request made by the infantes that he not permit the representatives of the Cid to use the swords Colada and Tizón (ll. 3538–58).

Finally, the heroes (the men representing the Cid) and the villains (the men of Carrión) duel in an open field (H^1). The three duels, another instance of trebling, take place diachronically. The first combat is between don Fernando and Pedro Bermúdez. The narrator details the pragmatographia of their struggle, recounting in vivid detail blows given and blows received:

Pero Vermúez,   el que antes rebtó,
con Ferrán Gonçález   de cara se juntó,
firiénse en los escudos   sin todo pavor.
Ferrán Gonçález a Pero Vermúez   el escudo l'
                                    passó,
prísol' en vazío,   en carne no l' tomó,
bien en dos logares   el astil le quebró.
Firme estido Pero Vermúdez,   por esso no
                                    s'encamó,
un colpe recibiera,   mas otro firió,
quebrantó la bloca del escudo,   a par ge la echó,
passógelo todo,   que nada no l' valió,
metiól' la lança por los pechos,   que nada no l'
                                    valió.
Tres dobles de loriga   tenié Fernando, aquesto l'
                                    prestó,
las dos le desmanchan   e la tercera fincó.
El belmez con la camisa   e con la guarnizón
de dentro en la carne   una mano ge lo metió.
                                    (ll. 3623–37)
[Pedro Bermúdez, who had issued the first challenge,
fought Fernando González face to face;
fearlessly they smote each other's shield.
Fernando González pierced Pedro Bermúdez's shield,
but his lance cut through empty space and did not
                                    strike flesh.
Indeed the shaft split in two places.
Pedro Bermúdez held firm and did not lose his
                                    balance.
He had received one blow, but now he struck another,
shattering and breaking through the boss of the
                                    shield,
which was split from side to side and gave Fernando
                                    no protection.
Pedro Bermúdez plunged his lance into Fernando's
    breast, for his shield did not protect him;
Fernando wore three layers of armour, and this saved

for two were torn open but the third remained him, unbroken. His quilted tunic with his shirt and his armour was driven a hand's length into his flesh."]

Don Fernando falls from his horse spitting blood: "por la boca afuera la sangre l' salió" (l. 3638) ["and from his mouth there flowed blood"]. Seeing Pedro Bermúdez approach him with his sword Tizón in hand to deliver the death blow, don Fernando declares himself defeated (I): "cuando lo vió Ferrán Gonçález, conuvo a Tizón, / antes qu'el colpe esperasse dixo: —¡Vençudo só! —/ Atorgárongelo los fieles, Pero Vermúez le dexó" (ll. 3643–45) ["when Fernando González saw it, he recognized Tizón. / Rather than wait for the blow, he said: 'I am beaten' / The judges agreed, and Pedro Bermúdez left him"].

The second struggle (H^1) is between don Diego González and Martín Antolínez. Immediately upon entering into combat, Martín Antolínez wounds don Diego with his sword Colada, damaging his headpiece: "ráxol' los pelos de la cabeça, bien a la carne llegava" (l. 3655) ["it tore the hair from his head and bit into his flesh"], and, then, he strikes another blow with the flat surface of his sword that causes don Diego to panic and flee from the field, leaving Martín Antolínez alone in the combat zone. King Alfonso declares Martín Antolínez the victor of this duel (I^1): "Essora dixo el rey: —Venid vós a mi compaña. / Por cuanto avedes fecho, vencida avedes esta batalla.—/ Otórgangelo los fieles, que dize verdadera palabra" (ll. 3668–70) ["Then the King said: 'Come and join my company. / By the way you have fought you have won this combat.' / The judges confirmed that he spoke the truth"].

The third battle (H^1) is between Asur González and Muño Gustioz. Wounded, Asur González falls from his horse and appears to be dying from his wounds: "al tirar de la lança en tierra lo echó, / vermejo salió el astil e la lança e el pendón: / todos se cuedan que ferido es de muert" (ll. 3686–88) ["and as he <Muño Gustioz> tugged at the lance he threw Asur González to the ground. / Shaft, lance and pennant all came out bright red. / They all thought Asur mortally wounded"]. At the request of Gonzalo Ansúrez, Asur González's father, Muño Gustioz, who is poised to plunge his lance into Asur González's chest, steps back, and the judges of the match declare the representative of the Cid the victor of this duel (I): "dixo Gonçalo Assúrez: —¡No·l' firgades, por Dios / ¡Vençudo es el campo cuando esto se acabó! — / Dixieron los fieles: —Esto oímos nós—" (ll. 3690–92) ["Gonzalo Ansúrez said: 'Do not strike him, for God's sake! / The combat has been won now that this is done.' / The judges said: 'We hear what you say'"].

Immediately following the duels, the three representatives of the Cid depart for Valencia ($\downarrow$). The narrator provides the aetiology of why they leave at night: "El rey a los de mio Cid de noche los enbió, / que no les diessen salto nin oviessen pavor" (ll. 3698–99) ["The King commanded My Cid's men to leave by night, / lest there should be any fear of their being attacked"]. In a spatial and temporal foreshortening passage, the narrator tells his reader that Pedro Bermúdez, Martín Antolínez, and Muño Gustioz later "travelled by day and night," and in the following line has the three men in Valencia by the side of the Cid ($\{\{\downarrow G^2\}$: "A guisa de menbrados, andan días e noches, / felos en Valencia con mio Cid el Campeador (ll. 3700–1) ["As prudent men, they travelled by day and night. / Behold them now in Valencia with My Cid the Battler!"]. Informed of their triple victories, the Cid proclaims his daughters avenged (K^4) and proceeds, "sin vergüença" (l. 3716) {"without shame"}, to marry his daughters to the infante of Navarre and to the infante of Aragón (W:):

Prísos' a la barba Ruy Díaz, so señor:
—¡Grado al rey del cielo, mis fijas vengadas son,
agora las ayan quitas heredades de Carrión!
¡Sin vergüença las casaré, o a qui pese o a qui
non!—
Andidieron en pleitos los de Navarra e de Aragón,
ovieron su ajunta con Alfonso el de León,
fizieron sus casamientos con don Elvira e con
doña Sol.
Los primeros fueron grandes, mas aquestos son
mijores,
a mayor ondra las casa que lo que primero fue.
¡Ved cuál ondra crece al que en buen ora nació
cuando señoras son sus fijas de Navarra e de
Aragón!

> Oy los reyes d'España   sos parientes son,
> a todos alcança ondra   por el que en buen ora
> nació. (ll. 3713–25)
>
> [Ruy Díaz, their lord, clasped his beard:
> "Thanks be to the King of Heaven that my daughters
> have been avenged.
> Now they may indeed enjoy, without impediment,
> their lands in Carrión!
> I shall marry them with no dishonour {without
> shame} and with no thought for the displeasure
> of some."
> The princes of Navarre and Aragón carried out their
> negotiations;
> they had their meeting with Alfonso of León;
> they were married to Doña Elvira and Doña Sol.
> The first alliances were great, but these were finer
> still;
> My Cid married his daughters more prestigiously than
> before.
> See how the reputation grew of the man born in a
> favoured hour,
> since his daughters were now the ladies of Navarre
> and Aragón!
> Now, the kings of Spain are of his line,
> and all gain in honour through the man born in a
> favoured hour.]

Thus, the *Cantar de Mio Cid* concludes, as the above lines indicate, with a final ironic twist. The narrator avers, without any hesitation whatsoever, that it is to the everlasting glory of King Alfonso as well as the infante of Navarre and the infante of Aragón that now they have become legally related to the family of the Cid.[4,5,6]

Conclusion

In his *Morphology of the Folktale*, Propp analyzed a particular type of Russian fairy tale, one whose fundamental content relied on the element of magic. His study of the Aarne-Thompson tale types 300 through 749 clearly indicates that these tales follow an orderly and uniform progression with respect to the syntagmatic presentation of diegetic functions. Dundes, in his introductory commentary to the second edition of the English translation of Propp's work, suggests that "Propp's analysis should be useful in analyzing the structure of literary forms (such as novels and plays), comic strips, motion-pictures and television plots" (*Morphology* xiv)—works that fall outside the domain of the folktale. More germane to the purpose of my study of the *Cantar de Mio Cid* is Dundes's invitation to apply the syntactical principles in Propp's *Morphology* to the epic genre. Dundes first notes "that the last portion of the *Odyssey* is strikingly similar to Propp's functions 23–31" and then inquires "what is the relationship of Propp's *Morphology* to the structure of epic?" (*Morphology* xiv). My morphological examination of the *Cantar de Mio Cid*, which to the best of my knowledge constitutes the first Proppian syntagmatic study of the nineteen tales that together make up the *Cantar de Mio Cid*, in part answers Dundes's broad inquiry. In short, my intrinsic, structural analysis of the *Cantar de Mio Cid* reveals that Propp's seminal work on the Russian fairy tale and the *Cantar de Mio Cid* are, to be sure, closely related. The reason they are so related indubitably lies in the fact that the *Cantar de Mio Cid* derives from folk fable. In this regard, the Mio Cid lore in the *Cantar de Mio Cid* constitutes an extended fairy tale.[1] Indeed, as I have shown, the syntagmatic structure of the nineteen tales that I have scrutinized in my study of the *Cantar de Mio Cid* fundamentally conforms to the diachronic development of functions that Propp prescribes in his *Morphology*. In this regard, my analysis highlights the formulaic, and consequently almost identical, repetition or cloning of functions—especially those related to battle scenes: C↑GHJIK (or K-). This is true in the majority of the moves in Tale 1, and it holds for other tales as well. The above formulaic composite of functions characterizes, to cite a few instances, Tale 4 (that of the king of Valencia); Tale 6 (that of the count of Barcelona); Tale 7, Move 1 (that of the anonymous offense undertaken by the forces from Valencia); Tale 8 (that of the king of Seville); and Tale 10 (that of the king of Morocco). Note, furthermore, the cloning of the basic core of functions: $aB^2C{\uparrow}G^2o\text{-}MN$, in all three moves of Tale 5. Gestures by the Cid to Regain the Good Will of King Alfonso. Finally, besides my structural investigation of the *Cantar de Mio Cid*, I have shown in other publications that Propp's insightful conclusions equally apply to such disparate narratives as the pre-Columbian mythological Quiche Maya text of the Popol Vuh and to the twelve tales, interwoven in an intricately designed temporal web, that together make up Miguel Ángel Asturias's *El Señor Presidente* (1946), the most significant diegetic creation in the genre of the novel in Spanish American literature of the first half of the twentieth century (see Himelblau 1987, 1999, 2000, 2002).

Is there any hypothetical explanation that might account for such a phenomenon? My analysis would seem to suggest that the human brain has created—and, indeed, can create—only a restricted number of pristine, core narrative structures; that all stories are variants of these said core narrative structures; and that this explains why the narrative linear sequence of events follows the same order in the Popol Vuh, in the *Cantar de Mio Cid*, and in Asturias's *El Señor Presidente*, as it does in the Russian fairy tales analyzed by Propp in his *Morphology*. Therefore, I would take issue with Svatava Pirkova-Jakobson's claim, as stated in her introduction to Propp's *Morphology*, that "it is just the archaic features of the Russian fairy tale that are its exclusive national trademark" (*Morphology* xix). From a morphological point of view, I should think that, in fairy tales, the more archaic the features, the less they would belong to the domain of any particular culture, that is, the more universal or uniform we would expect their syntagmatic structure to be, and this would apply to any literary diegesis, be it a story or novel. As Dundes points out in his new introduction to Propp's *Morphology*, certain aspects of Propp's morphological findings may well be "cross-culturally valid" (*Morphology* xiv).

In short, the result of my present structural inquiry of the *Cantar de Mio Cid* and of my previous publications on the Popol Vuh and on Asturias's *El Señor Presidente* strongly indicate that what Propp has discovered is the pristine, morphologic, core structure of narrative form from which subsequent diegetic schemes derive. While only future empirical studies of archaic and nonarchaic narratives will prove or disprove my reductionist conception of narrative structure, it is clear that my present analysis of the anonymous medieval epic *Cantar de Mio Cid* lends support to such a conclusion.[2]

Appendix

Tale 2: The Tale of Doña Jimena, the Wife of Rodrigo Díaz
This is a single-move tale that commences in Cantar I and ends in Cantar II. Tale 2 deals with doña Jimena's separation from her husband at the monastery Saint Peter of Cardeña in Castile and her subsequent reunion with the Cid many years later in Valencia. Following is the symbolic transcription of this brief narrative:

$$\alpha a:^6 BC\uparrow G^2 Qw^2$$

(The above symbolic transcription corresponds to the numerical functions: VIIIa, IX, X, XI, XV, XXVII, and XXXI.)
The initial situation of this diegesis depicts doña Jimena, who in the epic poem is a passive character, and her two preteen-age daughters, Elvira and Sol, lodged at the monastery of Saint Peter of Cardeña (α). This state of affairs assumes that King Alfonso has banished the Cid from his realm and that the Cid has placed his wife and daughters to reside at the monestary for the duration of his extradition. Thus doña Jimena, from the start, lacks having a normal family existence together with her husband and she lacks a homestead ($a:^6$). Her brief encounter with her husband at the monastery, as the Cid prepares to depart from Castile, and her prayer to the Lord for his future safety—on doña Jimena's deesis to Christ to protect the Cid, see below—constitute interludes of leave-taking. Don Rodrigo's absence puts neither her life nor her daughters' lives at risk. Many years transpire. Having conquered Valencia, the Cid obtains King Alfonso's consent to allow his family to join him. Minaya Álvar Fáñez informs doña Jimena and her daughters of this fact (B) and he and his entourage escort them on horseback to Valencia ($C\uparrow G^2$). Greeted with jubilation in Valencia, doña Jimena has become the queen of Valencia and of the surrounding area—the latter constitutes a variant of function XXVII, the recognition of the heroine (Q). Lastly, she obtains a permanent homestead and resumes her marital existence with her husband (w^2).

Tale 3: The Tale of Doña Elvira and Doña Sol, the Daughters of Doña Jimena and Rodrigo Díaz
This tale consists of four moves. Move 1 relates the separation and reunion of the daughters with their father in Valencia; Move 2 narrates their marriages to don Fernando and don Diego, the infantes of Carrión; Move 3 deals with their mistreatment and abandonment by their husbands in the forest of Corpes; and Move 4 refers in passing to their remarriages to the infante of Navarre and infante of Aragón.

Move 1 (Cantar I and Cantar II)
Move 1, deals with the separation of the daughters from the Cid and their subsequent reunion with their father in Valencia. Below is the symbolic transcription of this move:

$$\alpha a:^6 BC{\uparrow}G^2Qw^2 \text{ var.}$$

(The above symbolic transcription corresponds to the numerical functions: VIIIa, IX, X, XI, XV, XXVII, and XXXI.)

This diegesis commences with Elvira and Sol, the two preteen-age daughters of doña Jimena and the Cid, lodged at the monastery of Saint Peter of Cardeña with their mother (α). Thus, the two children, who in the epic poem are passive characters, have no home and lack a normal family existence with their father ($a:^6$). Many years transpire. Having conquered Valencia, the Cid obtains King Alfonso's consent to allow his family to join him. Minaya Álvar Fáñez informs the now grown doña Elvira and doña Sol of this fact (B), and he and his entourage escort them on horseback to Valencia ($C{\uparrow}G^2$). Greeted with jubilation in Valencia, doña Elvira and doña Sol have become the princesses of Valencia and its surrounding area—the latter constitutes a variant of function XXVII, the recognition of the heroine (Q). Lastly, they obtain a permanent home and resume a normal family relationship with their father, don Rodrigo (w^2 var.).

Move 2 (Cantar II)
Move 2 relates the marriage of doña Elvira and doña Sol to don Fernando and don Diego, the infantes of Carrión. The symbolic transcription of Move 2 follows:

a^1BCMNW^*

(The above symbolic transcription corresponds to the numerical functions: VIIIa, IX, X, XXV, XXVI, and XXXI.)

Move 2 begins with doña Elvira and doña Sol, the teenage daughters of don Rodrigo, lacking husbands (a^1). The Cid, who has just returned to Valencia after meeting with King Alfonso at the banks of the Tajo River to discuss the future civil status of his two daughters, informs doña Elvira and doña Sol that it is the king's expressed request and mandate that they wed the infantes of Carrión (B). The following day, both the civil and religious ceremonies take place in which Minaya Álvar Fáñez, in fulfillment of the difficult task that the Cid had assigned him, formally gives the hands of doña Elvira and doña Sol in marriage to don Fernando and don Diego ($CMNW^*$): the text does not specify who is to marry whom. These two last events liquidate the initial lack on the part of doña Elvira and doña Sol and bring Move 2 to a close.

Move 3 (Cantar III)

Move 3 narrates the mistreatment that doña Elvira and doña Sol receive in the forest of Corpes at the hands of their husbands, don Fernando and don Diego, the infantes of Carrión. The symbolic transcription of Move 3 follows:

$A^6\{B\}C\uparrow:G:^2\downarrow:M:\{\uparrow G:^2\}N:\{\downarrow\}$

(The above symbolic transcription corresponds to the numerical functions: VIII, {IX}, X, XI, XV, XX, XXV {XI, XV}, XXVI, and {XX}.)

This move commences with doña Elvira and doña Sol remaining in the woods of Corpes with don Fernando and don Diego while those in their entourage continue on their journey to Carrión. Here the infantes flog their wives and leave them behind, unconscious, to die (A^6). Félix Muñoz, a nephew of the Cid who has been accompanying his cousins to Carrión, witnesses the mistreatment of his cousins from a distance. Once the infantes leave, he dispatches himself to assist his cousins and successfully helps them to regain consciousness ({B}C). Subsequently, he puts the two women on his horse and takes them to the tower of doña Urraca ($\uparrow G^2$). Then he departs to San Sebastián to fetch Diego Téllez, a person who had previously served militarily under Minaya Álvar Fáñez. Félix Muñoz poses a difficult task to Diego Téllez, namely that he provide shelter for doña Elvira and doña Sol. Diego Téllez responds by allowing the young women to stay at his house (M:{↑G^2}N{↓}). Informed of what transpired at Corpes, the Cid assigns Minaya Álvar Fáñez and Pedro Bermúdez with the task (M) of fetching his daughters and bringing them back to Valencia (N)—tacit here are the functions of departure {↑} and spatial transference from one kingdom to another on horseback {G^2} as well their return {↓}. The two emissaries of don Rodrigo successfully accomplish both tasks (M{↑G:^{2}}{↓}N).

Move 4 (Cantar III)
Move 4 reports on the betrothal and remarriage of the Cid's daughters to the infante of Navarre and to the infante of Aragón. The symbolic transcription of Move 4 follows:

$$a^1BC↑\{↓\}G^2MNW:$$

(The above symbolic transcription corresponds to the numerical functions: VIIIa, IX, X, XI {XX}, XV, XXV, XXVI, and XXXI.)

Back in Valencia and with their marriages to the infantes of Carrión officially dissolved, doña Elvira and doña Sol once again lack husbands (a^1). As the Cid resolves his grievances against the infantes of Carrión before a court of nobles in Toledo, two messengers unexpectedly arrive—their appearance constitutes a deus ex machina event in that their presence constitutes an effect lacking a justified cause. One of the emissaries represents the infante of Navarre; the other represents the infante of Aragón. The messengers request that the Cid give the hands of doña Elvira and doña Sol in marriage to the infante of Navarre and the infante of Aragón (B): the text does not specify who is to marry whom. The Cid, obtaining permission to proceed in this matter from King Alfonso, departs from Toledo (↑)—in this instance the function departure (↑) assimilates that of return ({↓})—to return to Valencia (C↑{↓}G^2). Following the positive outcome of the duels in which three of his representatives defeat the infantes of Carrión and a representative of the latter (MN), don Rodrigo marries his daughters to the infante of Navarre and to the infante of Aragón. Thus doña Elvira and doña Sol become queens (W:) and are now directly related to the royal family of King Alfonso.

Doña Jimena's Prayer
Doña Jimena's prayer constitutes a deesis in which she seeks to direct Christ's future comportment toward her husband. In her perlocutionary speech doña Jimena formulates a request, one that harbors a plea, and which pursues two practical purposes. One is immediate; the other, mediate. On the one hand, she beseeches Christ to perform another miracle, after rehearsing some that He has performed in the past, namely, that of promptly providing divine protection for her husband as he ventures, exiled, into harm's way in lands hostile to Christian men. On the other, she solicits, as well, that Christ reunite them at some later date so that they may resume once again their blissful conjugal relationship: "—¡cuando oy nos partimos,   en vida nos faz juntar!—" (l. 365) ["'Since we are separated today, bring us together again in our lifetime'"].

From an aesthetic point of view, there are many stylistic features of doña Jimena's deesis that rivet the reader's attention on the words of her fervent petition. Her text contains an ample use of the figure polysyndeton "e"; it stresses the figure diazeugma, where one subject commands many verbs—for example, in her reference to Christ: "Fezist" / "fezist" / "prisist" [ll. 331–33], "salveste" / "salvest" / "andidiste" (ll. 339–43), "fezist" / "resucitest" / "dexeste" (ll. 345–47), "resucitest" / "fust" / "quebranteste" / "saqueste" / "eres" (ll. 358–61); in her reference to Longinus: "era" / "vio" / "diot' " (ll. 352–53), "alçó" / "llegó" / "abrió" / "cató" / "crovo" (ll. 355–57); and in her reference to her own person: "adoro" / "creo" / "ruego" (ll. 362–63). The effect of hammer-like blows results from doña Jimena's insistent use of the following figures: anaphora—for example, "salveste" / "salvest" (ll. 339–42), "en" / "en" (ll. 357–58) —; anaphora-prozeugma—for example, "Fezist" / "fezist" (ll. 331–332); and isocolon—for example, "a Jonás" / "a Daniel" / "al señor San Sabastián" / "a Santa Susaña" (ll. 339–42). Of considerable interest is the antithesis: "el uno es en paraíso,   ca el otro non entró allá" (l. 350), in that it serves to introduce the animated Longinus prosopographia—an apocryphal, folkloric account of an occurrence whose literary source possibly stems from John 19:34. In this prosopographia, doña Jimena has the reader's eyes move in a antithetical sweeping movement. First the eyes of the reader move upward, following the apocryphal centurion's lance as it pierces the thorax of Christ; then the reader's eyes move downward, following the blood streaming from the lance-pierced body of Christ onto the hands of the apocryphal centurion; and, lastly, the reader's eyes shift once more in an upward direction, following the apocryphal centurion's blood-stained hands rising to and then touching his blind eyes (ll. 352–56).

Other means by which doña Jimena accentuates her deesis is through the use of alliteration and interior rhyme. There is the repetition of the vowel "a" in line 337 ("Gaspar e Baltasar"), of the consonant sounds "s," "m," and "p" (in l. 342, l. 344, and l. 345, respectively), of the consonant sounds "f," "k" / "p," and the trill "rr" (in l. 359, l. 360, and l. 361, respectively). Note, also, the emphatic alliterative use of the vowel "e," in the line containing a prozeugma of the verb *ser*, in which doña Jimena emphasizes the all-powerful nature of Christ through the polyptoton "rey" / "reyes": "Tu eres rey de los reyes   e de tod el mundo padre" (l. 361) ["'You are the King of Kings and Father of the whole world'"].

Besides alliteration, interior rhyme, with its intrinsic emphasis on reiteration, plays a key role in creating and maintaining the emotional charge that doña Jimena projects so effectively in her deesis to Christ on behalf of her husband. In her delivery, she uses a minimum of eight different interior rhyme forms. These are: the assonant-paroxytone rhyme "a-o" ("grados" / "rogando" / "cuanto"); the consonant-oxytone rhyme "or" ("Criador" / "Campeador" / "Señor"); the consonant-paroxytone rhyme "elo" (in the ploce: "cielo" [Heaven] / "cielo" {firmament}); the assonant-paroxytone rhyme "e"-"o" ("cielo" / "tercero", "creo" / "ruego" / "Peidro"); the assonant-paroxytone rhyme "e-a" ("tierra" / "estrellas"); the assonant-oxytone rhyme stressing an "o" ("abrió" / "cató"); and the consonant-oxytone acute rhyme "ar" ("Gaspar" / "Baltasar").

To close this stylistic analysis of doña Jimena's plea, note the rare use in the *Cantar de Mio Cid* of the figure hypozeugma: "oro e tus e mirra te ofrecieron" (l. 338). Doña Jimena's deesis follows:

    Echós' doña Ximena en los grados delant altar,
    rogando al Criador,   cuanto ella mejor sabe,
    que a mio Cid el Campeador que Dios le curiás de
                  mal:
    —¡Ya Señor glorioso, Padre que en cielo estás!
    Fezist cielo e tierra,   el tercero el mar;
    fezist estrellas e luna, e el sol pora escalentar;

                    e ruego a San Peidro   que me ayude a rogar
                    por mio Cid el Campeador,   que Dios le curie de
                                                                   mal;
                    ¡cuando oy nos partimos,   en vida nos faz
                                                              juntar!— (ll. 327-65)
[Doña Jimena threw herself on the steps before the
                                                altar,
beseeching the Creator, with all her heart,
that he [*sic*] might keep My Cid the Battler from all
                                                 harm:
"O glorious Lord, Father in Heaven!
You made heaven and earth and then the sea;
you made stars and moon and the sun to give
                                            warmth.
You became flesh by Mary the Holy Mother;
you were born in Bethlehem according to your will.
Shepherds worshipped and praised you;
three kings came from Arabia to honour you —
Melchior and Caspar and Balthazar —
gold and frankincense and myrrh they offered you
                                      according to your will.
You saved Jonah when he fell into the sea;
you saved Daniel among the lions in the evil den;
you saved Saint Sebastian in Rome;
you saved Saint Susannah from the false accuser.
You walked on earth for thirty two years, heavenly
                                                Lord,
performing miracles which we talk of now;
from water you made wine and from the stone bread;
you raised Lazarus, as was your will.
You allowed yourself to be taken by the Jews and on
                                        Mount Calvary
they put you on a cross in the place called Golgotha.
Two thieves were with you on either side;
one is in Paradise, but the other did not enter there.
When on the cross, you performed a very great
                                             miracle:

prisist encarnación   en Santa María madre,
en Beleem aparecist,   commo fue tu voluntad,
pastores te glorificaron,   oviéronte a laudare,
tres reyes de Arabia   te vinieron adorar,
Melchior   e Gaspar e Baltasar
oro e tus e mirra te ofrecieron,   commo fue tu
                                           veluntad;
salveste a Jonás   cuando cayó en la mar,
salvest a Daniel   con los leones en la mala cárcel,
salvest dentro en Roma   al señor San Sabastián,
salvest a Santa Susaña   del falso criminal;
por tierra andidiste treinta e dos años,   Señor
                                              spirital,
mostrando los miráculos,   por én avemos qué
                                              fablar:
del agua fezist vino   e de la piedra pan,
resucitest a Lázaro,   ca fue tu voluntad,
a los judíos te dexeste prender;   do dizen monte
                                           Calvarie
pusiéronte en cruz,   por nombre en Golgotá,
dos ladrones contigo,   éstos de señas partes,
el uno es en paraíso,   ca el otro non entró allá;
estando en la cruz   vertud fezist muy grant:
Longinos era ciego,   que nuncuas vio alguandre,
diot' con la lança en el costado,   dont ixió la
                                           sangre,
corrió por el astil ayuso,   las manos se ovo de
                                           untar,
alçólas arriba,   llególas a la faz,
abrió los ojos,   cató a todas partes,
en ti crovo al ora,   por end es salvo de mal;
en el monumento resucitest   [. . . . .]
e fust a los infiernos,   commo fue tu voluntad,
quebranteste las puertas   e saqueste los santos
                                           padres.
Tú eres rey de los reyes   e de tod el mundo padre,
a ti adoro e creo   de toda voluntad,

Longinus was blind and had never had sight;
he thrust his lance into your side from where the blood flowed
down the shaft and covered his hands,
which he raised up to his face;
he opened his eyes, looked all around;
he believed in you from then and so was saved.
In the tomb you rose again;
you went down into Hell, according to your will,
broke down the gates and released the holy prophets.
You are King of Kings and Father of the whole world.
I worship you and believe in you with all my heart.
I pray to Saint Peter that he may intercede
for My Cid the Battler, that God may keep him from evil.
Since we are separated today, bring us together again in our lifetime."]

Tale 4: The King of Valencia's Counterattack against the Cid
This Moorish counteroffensive in Cantar I consists of a single-move tale. Its symbolic transcription follows:

$$\alpha a B^4 C \uparrow F^9 G^2 H^1 J:^1 I^1 - K^{10} -$$

(The above symbolic transcription corresponds to the numerical functions: VIIIa, IX, X, XI, XIV, XV, XVI, XVII, XVIII, and XIX.)

The initial situation (α) of this tale consists of the Moors of Ateca, Terrer, and Calatayut notifying King Tamín of Valencia, under whose political sphere and protection they reside, not only of the losses he has recently incurred at the hands of the Cid, which includes the fall of Alcocer, but also of the prospects of other immanent proleptic forfeitures unless he intervenes to free them from don Rodrigo's military incursions (aB^4). The king of Valencia immediately decides on counteraction (C) and sends an army of three thousand men to defeat the Cid under the joint command of King Fáriz and King Galve ($\uparrow F^9$). The troops, on horseback (and on foot), turn toward Alcocer—passing on land thus from one kingdom into another (G^2)—and set up a blockade of the city occupied by don Rodrigo. The blockade lasts for three weeks and exhausts the food and water supplies of the Cid, forcing don Rodrigo to engage the Moorish forces. The ensuing battle takes place in an open field (H^1). King Fáriz and King Galve receive serious wounds from don Rodrigo and Martín Antolínez, respectively (J^1:), and they lose the battle to the Cid's army of six hundred men (I^1-). Due to this defeat, King Tamín fails to liberate his captive vassals from their Christian conquerors (K^{10}-). The narrative passages dealing with the battle scenes constitute examples of enargia—that is, scenes of swift movement that vividly, and often grotesquely, depict hand-to-hand combat. In this battle, the Christian soldiers slay without pity their Moorish enemies and leave the battlefield strewn with mounds of dead Moorish bodies, many cut at the waist, and dead Moorish mounts as far as the eye can see.

Tale 5: Gestures by the Cid to Regain the Good Will of King Alfonso
This tale consists of three moves. Move 1 occurs after the Cid captures Alcocer; Move 2 takes place following the Cid's defense of Valencia, in which he defeats the Moorish king of Seville; and Move 3 follows his defeat of the Moroccan King Yúsuf who ventures onto Spanish soil in an attempt to reconquer Valencia from the Cid. Note that in these three overtures (a typical folkloric case of trebling), the Cid fails to obtain King Alfonso's pardon.

Move 1 (Cantar I)
The first attempt of reconciliation on the part of the Cid occurs after he defeats the army of three thousand men sent against him by King Támin, under the command of King Fáriz and King Galve, following his conquest of Alcocer. The symbolic transcription of Move 1 follows:

$$\alpha a B^2 C \uparrow \{ \underline{G^2} \} \S M \ \underline{N}\text{-}\{Q\}$$
$$\{ G^2 \downarrow \} \quad N$$

(The above symbolic transcription corresponds to the numerical functions: VIIIa, IX, X, XI, {XV}, XXV, XXVI, {XXVII}, and {XV, XX}.)
Having vanquished the forces of King Fáriz and King Galve at Alcocer (α), don Rodrigo informs Minaya Álvar Fáñez of his desire to dispatch him to King Alfonso so that he may: (1) inform the latter: "—que

me á airado—" (l. 815 [a]) ["'who has banished me'"], of what has transpired to his faithful vassal since he left Castile; and (2) to deliver to the king a gift of thirty fully equipped Arabic horses (B^2). Minaya Álvar Fáñez enthusiastically accepts this contract (C) and departs (↑) from Alcocer en route to Castile. A brief interlude ensues—an interlude that is synchronic to Minaya's trip to don Alfonso's court. In this interlude the narrator tells the reader that the Cid sells Alcocer for three thousand marks of silver to a consortium led by King Fáriz; he reveals the sadness expressed orally by the residents of the city over the immanent departure of the Cid from their castle; and, finally, he narrates don Rodrigo's subsequent departure (↑) and incursions in other Moorish territories (ll. 845–69). It is at this point that the narrator, foreshortening time and space, resumes the narrative of Minaya Álvar Fáñez's arrival at don Alfonso's court in Castile, thus rendering tacit his transference from one kingdom to another $\{G^2\}$. After delivering don Rodrigo's gifts to the monarch, Minaya Álvar Fáñez, in a connective segment, updates King Alfonso regarding the state of affairs of don Rodrigo during the latter's three weeks in exile (§) and then unsuccessfully intercedes before the king to pardon the Cid (MN-). Move 1 closes with King Alfonso returning to Minaya Álvar Fáñez his confiscated lands and decreeing that anyone in his kingdom who wishes to join the Cid may do so (N). By the latter decree, King Alfonso tacitly acknowledges the Cid as a hero {Q}. Lastly, Minaya Álvar Fáñez's return journey constitutes a tacit transference from one kingdom to another $\{G^2\downarrow\}$. At this point the narrator invokes the formulaic device of "meanwhile, back at the ranch": "Quiérovos dezir del que en buen hora cinxo espada" (l. 899) ["I want to tell you of the man who girded his sword in a favoured hour"]. With the latter phrase, the narrator then returns to covering the synchronic ventures of the Cid (Tale 1. Move 6).

Move 2 (Cantar II)
With the gains he obtained from defeating the king of Seville, the Cid decides to send Minaya Álvar Fáñez once again as his emissary to the court of King Alfonso. The symbolic transcription of Move 2 of Tale 5 follows:

$$aB^2C[D^7E^7F^9]\uparrow\{G^2\}\S LExM:N:\{Q\}\downarrow$$

(The above symbolic transcription corresponds to the numerical functions: VIIIa, IX, X [XII, XIII, XIV], XI, {XV}, XXIV, XXVIII, XXV, XXVI, {XXVII}, and XX.)

The Cid has yet to regain the favor of King Alfonso. Upon his victory over the king of Seville, don Rodrigo informs Minaya Álvar Fáñez of his desire to send him as his intermediary of goodwill to the Christian king with a gift of one hundred horses and to obtain don Alfonso's permission to allow his wife and two daughters to leave Castile and join him in Valencia (aB^2). Minaya Álvar Fáñez accepts this contract (C)": "—De buena voluntad.—" (l. 1282) ["'I am most willing'"]. As Minaya Álvar Fáñez prepares to take his leave, the narrator, in a deus ex machina passage—that is, in a passage that is totally unjustified from a structural point of view—introduces a new character, don Jerónimo, a bishop. The latter assumes the role of a donor and petitions don Rodrigo to allow him to engage in killing Moors "con sus manos" (l. 1294) ["hand to hand"], the infidel enemies of the Christian faith (D^7). (To indicate their deus ex machina aspect, the functions that apply to the incident between don Jerónimo and don Rodrigo appear in brackets.) The Cid not only complies with don Jerónimo's request ($[E^7]$), but he also puts himself at don Jerónimo's disposal ($[F^9]$), vowing that he will create a bishopric for him in Valencia. With these words still fresh in his memory, Minaya Álvar Fáñez exits Valencia (↑). At this juncture the narrator, in a passage that contains an apostrophe to the reader as well as a parelcon, foreshortens both space and time—that is, he renders function XV, the passing from one kingdom to another (G), tacit—: {G^2}: "[a]deliñó pora Castiella Minaya Álbar Fáñez; / dexarévos las posadas,   non las quiero contar" (ll. 1309–10) ["Minaya Álvar Fañez made for Castile. / I shall not describe the stages of his journey—I do not wish to tell of them"]. This places Minaya Álvar Fáñez directly in Castile and, subsequently, in Carrión where don Alfonso is residing. In a connective segment (§) that leads to the next function in this move, Minaya Álvar Fáñez updates the king regarding the Cid's most recent conquests; he informs the monarch that the Cid has amassed great wealth; and he delivers don Rodrigo's gifts to King Alfonso. These actions instill a strong swell of jealousy in Count Garci Ordóñez, a noble in don Alfonso's retinue, who without constraint reacts negatively, presenting a false claim against the Cid (L): "—¡Semeja que en tierra de moros   non á bivo omne / cuando assí faze a su guisa   el Cid Campeador!—" (ll. 1346–47) ["'It seems that in the land of the Moors there is no one left living, / since our Cid the Battler has everything his own way'"]. His commentary, in turn, elicits an immediate, sharp, and caustic rebuke from the monarch, which exposes the false hero and brands him as a villain (Ex): "Dixo el rey al conde: —¡Dexad essa razón, / que en todas guisas   mijor me sirve que vós!—" (ll. 1348–49) ["The King said to the Count: 'Be silent! / For in any case, he serves me better than you'"]. What follows is Minaya Álvar Fáñez's plea to the king that he consent to the Cid's family rejoining don Rodrigo in Valencia, a request that poses a difficult task for the king (M). Don Alfonso approves don Rodrigo's petition (N), declaring, furthermore, that any individual presently serving under him may now enlist in the Cid's ranks (N): "—Los que quisieren ir   servir al Campeador / de mí sean quitos e vayan   a la gracia del Criador—" (ll. 1369–70) ["'Those who wish to leave to serve the Battler / I make free of their obligation to me; let them go with the grace of God'"]. King Alfonso's words tacitly acknowledge, once more, that the Cid is a hero {Q}.

Move 2 of Tale 5 reaches its structural moment of auxesis with the drawn-out episode of the Cid's wife and his two daughters leaving the monastery and joining the Cid in Valencia, a journey that forms part of the aforementioned difficult task and its resolution (MN↓).

Move 3 (Cantar II)

Having defeated King Yúsuf of Morocco, the Cid once again seeks to inform King Alfonso of his latest exploits. The symbolic transcription of this third and final attempt to regain the favor of his sovereign follows below:

$$aB^1[D^7F^{1,\,9}]C\uparrow G^2MNL\{Q\}T^3$$

(The above symbolic transcription corresponds to the numerical functions: VIIIa, IX, [XII, XIV], X, XI, XV, XXV, XXVI, XXIV, {XXVII}, and XXIX.)

Reunited with his family, the Cid, however, has yet to regain his position of confidence and trust with King Alfonso (a). The latter leads the Cid to attempt for the third and last time to seek his king's pardon. The Cid assigns Minaya Álvar Fáñez and Pedro Bermúdez as his goodwill ambassadors to the king and charges them to relate to the king his latest victories and to give him a present of two hundred horses "—con siellas e con frenos   e con señas espadas—" (l. 1810) ["'with saddles, bridles, and each with a sword'"]. (Note that don Rodrigo here assimilates function IX: Mediation [B^1], with that of function XII: Donor [D^7], and with that of function XIV: that of a character who not only transfers a gift, but who also puts himself at the disposition of the hero [$F^{1, 9}$]. In the case of the Cid, the latter's hero is King Alfonso.) Both Minaya Álvar Fáñez and Pedro Bermúdez accept the above contract and take their leave of don Rodrigo (C↑). They travel continuously during "los días e las noches" (l. 1823) {"by day and by night"} and cross "la sierra   que las otras tierras parte" (l. 1824) ["They crossed the mountains which separated them from the kingdom of Castile"] and, following a brief search, locate the king in Valladolid (G^2). Greeted warmly by don Alfonso, they inform him of the Cid's latest ventures and they fulfill the difficult task that the Cid has assigned them, namely, to place in the king's hands his gift of two hundred horses (MN). The military success of don Rodrigo, in turn, leads Count García and his relatives, in an aside, to utter a false claim against the Cid (L):

> Pesó al conde don García   e mal era irado,
> con diez de sos parientes   aparte davan salto:
> —¡Maravilla es del Cid,   que su ondra crece tanto!
> En la ondra que él ha   nós seremos abiltados;
> por tan biltadamientre   vencer reyes del campo,
> commo si los fallasse muertos   aduzirse los
>   cavallos,
> por esto que él faze   nós avremos enbargo.—
>   (ll. 1859–65)
> [But this grieved Count Don García, who was very
>   angry;
> with ten of his kinsmen he drew to one side:
> "It is a marvel that the Cid's reputation grows so
>   much.
> By his increasing honour, we shall lose our credit.
> In so basely overcoming kings on the field of battle,

as if he found them dead he brings their horses as evidence. Because of what he does, there will be trouble for us."]

The king's acceptance of the Cid's gift tacitly indicates that the king acknowledges the Cid as a hero {Q}. Finally, don Alfonso effects a transfiguration in both Minaya Álvar Fáñez and Pedro Bermúdez by ordering that they not only be dressed in new clothes, but also be given new arms (T^3).

Tale 6: The Failure of Ramón Berenguer, Count of Barcelona, to Regain Lands Lost to the Cid
The symbolic transcription of this single-move tale in Cantar I, depicting the failure of don Ramón, count of Barcelona, to defeat the Cid at or near the vicinity of Tévar, follows:

$$\alpha\zeta aB^3C\uparrow G^2H^1I^1\text{-}K^4\text{-}M\underline{N}\text{-}\{Q\}U\text{-}N$$

(The above symbolic transcription corresponds to the numerical functions: V, VIIIa, IX, X, XI, XV, XVI, XVIII, XIX, XXV, XXVI, {XXVII}, and XXX.)

The initial situation (α) introduces the figure of don Ramón Berenguer, count of Barcelona, and continues with function V: Delivery (ζ), that is, with the Frank receiving news of the Cid's incursions and gains into areas in and around Zaragoza that are under his direct sphere of political and military influence. Don Rodrigo's conquests constitute, clearly, a loss for don Ramón, a lack (a) that adds injury to an insult that the Cid had previously inflicted upon the count of Barcelona when, in the latter's court, he had wounded the count's nephew (B^4). Riled, the Frank decides to counteract (C) and, with an army formed of Christians and Moors, leaves his residence ($\uparrow$), passing through diverse territories until he encounters the Cid in the vicinity of Tévar (G^2). Here don Rodrigo engages the count in battle, defeats him, and takes him prisoner (H^1I^1-), thus impeding don Ramón's ability to be victorious (K^4-). Confronted with a difficult task, that of breaking bread with the Cid at the latter's table (M), don Ramón initially first refuses to submit to the Cid's request (N-): "—

Non combré un bocado   por cuanto ha en toda España, / antes perderé el cuerpo   e dexaré el alma— (ll. 1021–22) ["'I will not eat a mouthful, for all the wealth in Spain; / I would rather die and give up my soul'"]. Subsequently, however, after the Cid gives don Ramón his word that he will release him and his two noble compatriots, the count of Barcelona acquiesces to the Cid's demand (N). By dining at the Cid's table, the count tacitly acknowledges don Rodrigo as a hero {Q} and avoids punishment to his person and his men (U-)—that is, of remaining captives of the Cid.

Tale 7: The Reaction of the Residents of Valencia against the Cid

This is a two-move tale that occurs in Cantar II.

Move 1 (Cantar II)
Move 1 marks the reaction of the inhabitants of Valencia to the Cid's latest triumphs. The symbolic transcription of Move 1 of this double-move tale follows:

$$\alpha a B^3 C \uparrow G^2 H^1 I^1 \text{-} K \text{-} \downarrow PsRs \text{ var.}$$

(The above symbolic transcription corresponds to the numerical functions: VIIIa, IX, X, XI, XV, XVI, XVIII, XIX, XX, XXI, and XXII.)

The Cid's latest exploits in territories adjacent to Valencia constitute the initial situation of this move (α). Due to don Rodrigo's military excursions, the residents of Valencia feel insecure (a) —they openly discuss among themselves their lack of security (B^3). The residents decide it is in their best interest to launch a preemptive attack on the forces of don Rodrigo (C). They leave their city ($\uparrow$) and travel on horseback by night to Murviedro, where the Cid resides (G^2). After four days they find themselves under attack by the Cid's army (H^1); they fare poorly at the hands of the forces of don Rodrigo (I^1-) and, thereby, fail to cure their initial lack (K^4-). They flee ($\downarrow$), pursued by the Cid's men (Pr), but they manage to return to Valencia where they find safe haven within their city's gates (Rs var.).

Move 2 (Cantar II)
Move 2 deals with the immediate social state of affairs that follow after the residents of Valencia fail to defeat the Cid. The symbolic

transcription of Move 2 follows:

$$a\ B^4C\text{-}K^4\text{-}$$

(The above symbolic transcription corresponds to the numerical functions: VIIIa, IX, X, and XIX.) Trapped within the walls of Valencia, the inhabitants find themselves in a state of turmoil. The community borders on anarchy for the inhabitants appear to have lost their moral bearings, resulting in a lack of law and order as well as a lack of mutual trust (a). One surmises the existence of such a social state of affairs from the omniscient narrator's rhetorical manipulation of language. To this end he makes effective use of the figures prozeugma (of the conjugated verb *dar*), polysyndeton (of the conjunction "nin"), antimetabole ("padre a fijo"-"fijo a padre"), and diacope ("amigo a amigo"), closing with an apostrophe to the reader, an expression of pathos in which the omniscient narrator commiserates with the unfortunate residents who are dying of famine. Note that the omniscient narrator makes his illocutionary assertions using the predominantly present tense of the indicative mood that characterizes authorial commentary: "Nin da consejo padre a fijo   nin fijo a padre/ nin amigo a amigo   no's' pueden consolar" (ll. 1176–77). The pertinent passage follows:

>   Mal se aquexan los de Valencia,   que non sabent
>   qué's' far,
>   de ninguna part que sea   non les vinié pan.
>   Nin da consejo padre a fijo   nin fijo a padre,
>   nin amigo a amigo   nos' pueden consolar.
>   ¡Mala cueta es, señores,   aver mingua de pan,
>   fijos e mugieres   verlos murir de fanbre!
>   (ll. 1174–79)
>   [The people of Valencia bitterly lamented—they
>   knew not what to do:
>   from nowhere could they get food.
>   Father could not aid son nor son help father,
>   nor could friend bring consolation to friend.
>   It is a harsh fate, my lords, to have not enough to eat,
>   and to see women and children dying of hunger.]

The residents of Valencia seek outside assistance by notifying the king of Morocco of their plight (B^4), but the king, engaged militarily elsewhere at the time, is unable to come to their assistance (C-). Insecurity and turmoil continue to reign among the inhabitants of Valencia. The Cid lays siege to the city for nine months. On the tenth month, the residents of Valencia, unable to resolve their state of affairs, decide to capitulate (K^4-).

Tale 8: The Failure of the King of Seville to Retake Valencia
The fall of Valencia triggers a military response on the part of the king of Seville. The symbolic transcription of this single-move tale in Cantar II follows:

$$\alpha a B^3 C \uparrow \{G^2\} H^1 J : {}^1\text{-}I^1\text{-}K\text{-}\downarrow$$

(The above symbolic transcription corresponds to the numerical functions: VIIIa, IX, X, XI, {XV}, XVI, XVII, XVIII, XIX, and XX.)

The initial situation (α) reveals that the king of Seville has received news of the fall of Valencia to the forces of the Cid. To regain the city, the loss of which constitutes a lack (a) for the king of Seville, the Moorish monarch gathers an army of thirty thousand men and undertakes an offensive counteraction against the Cid, dispatching himself and his forces forthwith to Valencia (a $B^3C\uparrow$). The next instant, which constitutes an evident case of foreshortening of both time and space, finds the king of Seville in the vicinity of Valencia—the latter renders function XV: the crossing from one kingdom to another on land tacit: ($\{G^2\}$). The two factions engage in a battle in an open field; the king of Seville receives three wounds (another typical, folkloric case of trebling) from the sword of the Cid; he meets defeat at the hands of don Rodrigo, which leaves his initial lack intact, yet somehow manages to escape ($H^1 J : {}^1\text{-}I^1\text{-}K\text{-}\downarrow$).

Tale 9: The Tale of Raquel and Vidas
This tale, which consists of two moves, involves two Jewish businessmen who lend monies to the Cid in his hour of greatest need.

Move 1 (Cantar I)
The symbolic transcription of Move 1 follows:

αβε{ζ}η:θ:a:⁵C↑↓DEF
(The above symbolic transcription corresponds to the numerical functions: I, IV, {V}, VI,VII, VIIIa, X, XI, XX, XII, XIII, and XIV.) The initial situation (α) reflects the Cid's need to obtain monies to support himself as well as the men who have decided to follow him into exile. To this end the Cid, as I pointed out in Tale 1: Move 2, assumes the role of a villain and consciously—that is, by an act of proairesis—recruits Martín Antolínez to help him take advantage of two Jewish businessmen. Don Rodrigo asks Martín Antolínez to assist him in committing the sin of fraud against two innocent persons, Raquel and Vidas. (In passing I should point out that the sin of fraud is a most grievous one. It is a sin of the intellect, a sin against the greatest gift that God has bestowed on man— that is, the gift of reason, a gift that God gave to man to distinguish him from the other beings in the animal kingdom, a gift that God gave to man so that he would be a creature after the likeness, in the image, of his Creator.) Adapting himself comfortably in this satanic role, Martín Antolínez departs from the Cid's camp outside of Burgos (β), enters Burgos, and inquires as to the whereabouts of Raquel and Vidas (ε): "Passó por Burgos, al castiello entrava, / por Rachel e Vidas apriessa demandava" (ll. 98–99) ["He made his way through Burgos and entered the castle, / asking urgently for Raquel and Vidas"].

Once Martín Antolínez finds them (function V. Delivery, is tacit {ζ}), he, proairetically—that is, by deliberate choice—lies to them. He avers that the Cid possesses two chests that contain gold: "—Tiene dos arcas llenas de oro esmerado—" (l. 113) ["'He has two chests full of pure gold'"], when they contain only sand. He relates that circumstances force the Cid to pawn those chests as surety to Raquel and Vidas: "—el Campeador dexarlas ha en vuestra mano, / e prestalde de aver lo que sea guisado—" (ll. 117–18) ["'The Battler will entrust them into your hands; / you are to lend him as much money as would be appropriate'"]. Martín Antolínez succeeds in his villainous trickery (η) and gets Raquel and Vidas, who fall victims to his deceit (θ), to agree to lend the Cid six hundred marks. (Interestingly, it neither occurs to Raquel and Vidas to question the sum asked of them nor to haggle over it.) The agreed-upon monies of the loan create, in principle, a financial lack for Raquel and Vidas (a^5). With the Cid's promise still ringing in their ears—namely, that they will lack for nothing during their lifetime for having done him this favor (η): "—mientra que vivades   non seredes menguados—" (l. 158) ["'as long as you live you will never be in need'"]—Raquel and Vidas return to their place of business with the chests filled with sand (C↑↓). At their abode, they fulfill their part of the contract and transfer to Martín Antolínez the stipulated, and agreed upon amount—thereby concretely substantiating the above lack for themselves (a^5). In addition, they confer upon Martín Antolínez a commission, one that Martín Antolínez does not hesitate to accept, for his part in having brokered this business transaction (DEF). (Regarding folk-motif designations here, see Chapter 3, notes 5 and 6.)

Move 2 (Cantar II)
Below is the symbolic transcription of Move 2:

$$a^5BC$$

(The above symbolic transcription corresponds to the numerical functions: VIIIa, IX, and X.)

Years have elapsed and the Cid, apparently, has never made good on his word as a Christian. At the moment when doña Jimena and her daughters prepare to leave the monastery of Saint Peter of Cardeña to join the Cid in Valencia, Raquel and Vidas resurface in the diegesis to inform Minaya Álvar Fáñez that the Cid has caused them to suffer a serious economic loss (a^5). They petition him to intervene before the Cid on their behalf to see that don Rodrigo repays the loan of six hundred marks (B): "—¡Merced, Minaya,   cavallero de prestar! / ¡Desfechos nos ha el Cid,   sabet, si no nos val! / Soltariemos la ganancia,   que nos diesse el cabdal—"(ll. 1432–34) ["'A favour, Minaya, worthy knight! / Unless he helps us now, the Cid has ruined us; / we would forget about the interest, if only he would give us back the capital'"]. Minaya Álvar Fáñez, assuming the role of a hero, commits himself to their cause (C): "—Yo lo veré con el Cid   si Dios me lieva allá; / por lo que avedes fecho   buen cosiment ý avrá—" (ll. 1435–36) ["'I will ask the Cid about it, if God takes me safely to him; / there will be a good reward for what you have done'"]. As the matter stands, the above topic, in this poorly structured tale, ends in an ellipsis—that is, in Move 2 of Tale 9 the narrator neither mentions the subject of the loan again nor has the figures of Raquel and Vidas reappear in the epic poem. (Goldberg [118–19] fails to list this folk motif of breaking a promise under M205.)

> Tale 10: The Failure of King Yúsuf of Morocco to Recapture Valencia
> King Yúsuf of Morocco decides to recuperate the lands that the Cid has usurped from him. The symbolic transcription of this single-move tale in Cantar II follows:
>
> $$aC\uparrow\{G^2\}H^1J∺{}^1I^1\text{-}K\text{-}\downarrow var.$$
>
> (The above symbolic transcription corresponds to the numerical functions: VIIIa, X, XI, XV, XVI, XVII, XVIII, XIX, and XX.)
>
> Irate over the losses he has incurred in Spain, King Yúsuf of Morocco decides to engage the Cid in battle in order to recover Valencia (aC). In a passage that constitutes a foreshortening of time and space, the narrator tells of his departure from Morocco ($\uparrow$), his crossing the Strait of Gibraltar with an army of fifty thousand men, and his tacit setting up camp at the outskirts of Valencia $\{G^2\}$. Don Rodrigo, in turn, with just under four thousand men, launches a preemptive surprise counterattack (H^1). In the course of the battle he wounds Yúsuf three times ($J∺{}^1$) and defeats the king of Morocco (I^1-). Although he fails to liquidate his above initial lack (K^4-), the king of Morocco escapes with his life, finding refuge in a castle in Cullera ($\downarrow$var.).

> Tale 12: The Tale of the Cid's Handling of the Loose Lion Incident
> This is a single-move tale in Cantar III seen from the perspective of the Cid. Below is the symbolic transcription of the above move:
>
> $$\alpha a^6BCH^1\,var.\{M\}I\{N\}K^4$$
>
> (The above symbolic transcription corresponds to the numerical functions: VIIIa, IX, X, XVI {XXV}, XVIII {XXVI}, and XIX.)
>
> The initial situation of this single-move tale begins with a loose lion on the palace grounds (α). This fact places the Cid's life in peril. Although men from his retinue stand around him as a shield to protect him, the Cid still lacks assurance for his life (a^6). To remedy the present

misfortune requires that the Cid's men or don Rodrigo himself catch the lion and place the wild beast of prey back in its cage. The Cid, on a bench, awakens from his nap to find his men standing around him. His knights inform don Rodrigo of the situation at hand (B): "—¡Ya señor ondrado, rebata nos dio el león!— " (l. 2295) ["'Honoured lord, the lion filled us with terror'"]. The Cid decides upon counteraction (C) and directly engages the lion (H^1 var.) —his action assimilates function XXV: a difficult task {M}: "Mio Cid fincó el cobdo, en pie se levantó, / el manto trae al cuello e adeliñó pora'l león" (ll. 2296–97) ["My Cid sat up, leaning on his elbow, and then rose to his feet; / with his cloak fastened on his shoulders, he went towards the lion"]. The lion immediately submits to him, symbolically indicating that even Nature submits to the Cid: "el león, cuando lo vio, assí envergonçó, / ante mio Cid la cabeça premió e el rostro fincó" (ll. 2298–99) ["When it saw him, the lion felt such shame / that before My Cid it lowered its head and looked to the ground"]. Next, the Cid takes the lion by his nape and puts him back into his cage (I)—his action assimilates function XXVI: solution of a difficult task ({N}): "Mio Cid don Rodrigo al cuello lo tomó / e liévalo adestrando, en la red le metió" (ll. 2300–1) ["My Cid Don Rodrigo took it by the neck, / and, leading it along on his right hand side, put it in the cage"]. The latter does away with the lack of this move (K^4). (The Cid's handling of the lion constitutes a Spanish medieval folkloric motif; Goldberg 27, D2156.13].)

Tale 13: The Tale of the Cid's Victory over the Moroccan King Búcar
This is a single-move tale in Cantar III of the battle with King Búcar from the vantage point of the Cid. Following is the symbolic transcription of Move 1:

$$\alpha A^{19} BC\uparrow :H:^1[Pr-]I^1K^4\downarrow w^o$$

(The above symbolic transcription corresponds to the numerical functions: VIII, IX, X, XI, XVI, [XXI], XVIII, XIX, XX, and XXXI.)

This single-move tale begins with an initial situation (α) that, at the same time, constitutes a villainy (A). King Búcar of Morocco and his forces have pitched fifty thousand tents around Valencia and, in what amounts to a declaration of war against the Cid, have laid siege to the city

(A^{19}). Don Rodrigo and his men—with the exception of the infantes of Carrión—are ecstatic over this new opportunity to increase their wealth and look forward to doing battle with the Moors (BC). Instead of waiting for King Búcar to attack the city—the loud drum roll from the enemy camp indicates that a Moorish attack is imminent—the Spaniards leave Valencia (↑) and initiate the attack in an open field, devastating the Moorish cavalry and foot soldiers (H^1). In the passage below, of interest is the manner in which the narrator creates a vivid pragmatographia. To this end he employs the following figures: antimetabole ("de las tiendas los sacan" / "Sácanlos de las tiendas"); polyptoton ("tantos" / "tantas"); isocolon ("tanto braço" / "tantas cabeças"); prozeugma-apostrophe ("veriedes"); and alliteration of the consonant sound "k" and of the vowel "a" ("sacan" / "Sácanlos" / "cáenlos" / "alcaz"). The passage, besides, contains an apostrophe to the reader ("veriedes") to secure further the attention of the reader:

> Los de mio Cid a los de Bucar   de las tiendas los sacan.
> Sácanlos de las tiendas,   cáenlos en alcaz,
> tanto braço con loriga   veriedes caer apart,
> tantas cabeças con yelmos   que por al campo caen,
> cavallos sin dueños   salir a todas partes.
> (ll. 2402–6)
> [My Cid's troops drove Búcar's men out from their tents.
> They drove them from their tents and began the pursuit;
> you could see so many arms hewn off with their armour,
> so many helmeted heads falling to the ground,
> and riderless horses galloping off in all directions.]

The Cid pursues King Búcar on horseback—the direct combat with the enemy (H^1) here assimilates function XXI: pursuit, except that it is the pursuit of the enemy and not that of the hero [Pr-]. Catching up with the Moor close to the shoreline of the Mediterranean Sea, don Rodrigo strikes a vertical blow to his headpiece and splits King Búcar's body in two down to his waist. The narrator's enargia contains more than a hint of the grotesque (H:¹[Pr-]I¹):

> Alcançólo el Cid a Bucar a tres braças del mar,
> arriba alçó Colada, un grant colpe dado'l' ha,
> las carbonclas del yermo tollidas ge las ha,
> cortól' el yelmo e, librado todo lo ál,
> fata la cintura el espada llegado ha. (ll. 2420–24)
> [My Cid reached Búcar, three arm's lengths from
> the sea,
> and, raising Colada aloft, dealt him a mighty blow;
> he cut through the gems of the helmet;
> passing through the helmet and cutting everything
> else away,
> the sword sliced through him down to the waist.]

With the battle won, the Cid and his men return to the city ($\downarrow$). Afterward, not only do they share among themselves their newly acquired wealth—the Cid, in killing King Búcar has obtained for himself the Moor's sword Tizón—but also joyously celebrate the outcome of the battle (K^4 w°).

Tale 14: The Tale of the Attempt by the Moroccan King Búcar to Reconquer Valencia

The symbolic transcription of this single-move tale in Cantar III is as follows:

$$\{\alpha\}aBC\text{-}\uparrow\text{-}H\text{-}I\text{-}Pr\{K^{4\text{-}}\}$$

(The above symbolic transcription corresponds to the numerical functions: VIIIa, IX, X, XI, XVI, XVIII, XXI, and {XIX}.)

This single-move tale is a deus ex machina narrative. The narrator of the *Cantar de Mio Cid* does not provide an antecedent to justify this new attempt by a Moorish king to reconquer Valencia. (Coming immediately after the lion episode, one can perhaps take for granted that the narrator introduces this narrative to reemphasize the cowardly nature of the infantes of Carrión.) The initial situation of this diegesis, which constitutes a foreshortening of space and time, is tacit in that it assumes that King Búcar left Morocco, that he crossed the sea to reach Spain, that he marched to Valencia, and that, upon arriving at Valencia, he pitched his tents and laid siege to the city $\{\alpha\}$. The diegesis opens with a lack (a^6) — that is, the Moorish King Búcar's need to reconquer Valencia. From their pitched tents—the number of tents given constitutes a hyperbole: "cincuaenta mill tiendas fincadas ha de las cabdales" (l. 2313) ["they pitched fifty thousand large tents"]—the Moors announce their plan to attack the city immediately by beating their drums loudly (B). To the startling surprise of the Moors, it is the Cid and his knights who exit Valencia to engage them in battle (C-↑-). The Moorish forces are no challenge to the Cid and his army and King Búcar and his forces fail to reconquer Valencia. The heroes of this tale, the Moors, die in multitudes. King Búcar finds himself pursued (Pr) by the Cid and dies at his hands, his head and neck and torso partitioned vertically to his waist near the shore of the Mediterranean Sea (H-I-Pr$\{K^4_-\}$).

Tale 15: The Tale of the Moor Abengalbón's Encounter with the Infantes of Carrión.

Below is the symbolic transcription of the Abengalbón single-move tale that develops in Cantar III:

$$\alpha aC\uparrow G^2 DFL\text{-}MNEx\downarrow$$

(The above symbolic transcription corresponds to the numerical functions: VIIIa, X, XI, XV, XII, XIV, XXIV, XXV, XXVI, XXVIII, and XX.)

Abengalbón's meeting with the infantes constitutes a single-move tale. Having observed omens that portend negatively regarding the marriages of his two daughters to the infantes of Carrión, the Cid sends his nephew, Félix Muñoz, to accompany the infantes' entourage to see that his daughters reach Carrión safely. To this end, he instructs his nephew to request that Abengalbón, his Moorish friend in Molina, accompany the group to Medina—the above constitutes the initial situation (α) of this tale. When the infantes' entourage reaches Molina, Abengalbón sets out to fulfill the Cid's request, a request that until it is completed constitutes a lack for the Moor (a). Accompanied by two hundred of his horsemen, Abengalbón greets the infantes and their wives and escorts them the next day to Ansarera (C↑G^2). In Ansarera he assumes the role of a donor and gives unspecified gifts to doña Elvira and doña Sol and two horses to don Fernando and don Diego (DF): "A las fijas del Cid   el moro sus donas dio, / buenos seños cavallos   a los ifantes de Carrión" (ll. 2654–55) ["The Moor made his gifts to the Cid's daughters, / and gave fine horses to each of the Infantes of Carrión"]. Informed that the infantes intend to assassinate him (L-), Abengalbón undertakes the difficult task of directly confronting his enemies (M). He accomplishes the task (N) by delivering an oral lashing to don Fernando and don Diego, thereby exposing the infantes as villains (Ex). Of interest in Abengalbón's discourse below is his pseudo use of figure anacoenosis, which turns out to be a hypophora-epiplexis—that is, a question asked of another but answered by the addresser and raised not to solicit an answer, but rather to reproach the addressee. Also of interest, is the use of the figure antithesis in line 2680 and that of cataplexis—that is, the expression of a harsh and adamant warning—in line 2678:

—Dezidme,   ¿qué vos fiz, ifantes?
Yo sirviéndovos sin art   e vós, pora mí, muert
consejastes.
Si no lo dexás   por mio Cid el de Bivar,
tal cosa vos faría   que por el mundo sonás,
e luego levaría sus fijas   al Campeador leal.
¡Vós nuncua en Carrión   entrariedes jamás!—
(ll. 2675–80)
["Tell me what I have done to you, Infantes of
Carrión.
Though I served you without malice, you plotted
my death.
Were I not to hold back on account of My Cid of
Vivar,
I would do such a thing to you that the news of it
would echo throughout the world
and then I would take back to the loyal Battler his
daughters.
You would never re-enter Carrión!]

Following these words, Abengalbón takes his leave of the Infantes and returns to Molina (↓).

Tale 17: The Tale of King Alfonso
Tale 17 consists of two moves. Move 1 entails actions that are pertinent to Cantar I and Cantar II; Move 2 deals with the action that involves the Cid's revenge on the infantes of Carrión in Cantar III.

Move 1 (Cantar I and Cantar II)
Below is the symbolic transcription of Move 1:

$$\{A^9\}BD : E : F : {}^1K^4Qw^1$$

(The above symbolic transcription corresponds to the numerical functions: {VIII}, IX, XII, XIII, XIV, XIX, XXVII, and XXXI.)

So as to not rehearse the text of the Crónica de Veinte Reyes, I shall begin the tale of King Alfonso at the point where the latter has already banished the Cid—the sentence of expulsion is, thereby, tacit—from his realm ($\{A^9\}$), allowing him nine days to leave the territories under his sphere of influence. King Alfonso sends notice of his decision to ostracize the Cid throughout his realm and prohibits his subjects from harboring the Cid and his men (B). The Cid, conquering lands from Moors, sends the king presents (D :), gifts that King Alfonso welcomes (E : F : ^{1}). Following the battle with the Moroccan King Yúsuf, the king meets with the Cid to discuss the matrimony of his two daughters to the infantes of Carrión. At this time, King Alfonso pardons the Cid and accepts him as his vassal (K^4): "—Aquí vos perdono   e dóvos mi amor / e en todo mio reino   parte desde oy—" (ll. 2034–35) ["'Here and now I pardon you and grant you my love, / and from today I give you a place in my kingdom'"]. King Alfonso's pardon represents the official and public recognition that the Cid is a hero (Q). Subsequently, King Alfonso publicly orders the Cid to marry his two daughters to the infantes of Carrión (w^1) —for the folk-motif designation of this regal act, see Chapter 4, note 1—:

—¡Oídme, las escuelas,   cuende s e ifançones!
Cometer quiero un ruego   a mio Cid el Campeador,

assí lo mande Christus   que sea a so pro:
vuestras fijas vos pido,   don Elvira e doña Sol,
que las dedes por mugieres   a los ifantes de
                                                    Carrión.
Seméjam' el casamiento   ondrado e con grant pro,
ellos vos las piden   e mándovoslo yo.
D'ella e d'ella parte   cuantos que aquí son,
los míos e los vuestros,   que sean rogadores:
¡dándoslas, mio Cid,   sí vos vala el Criador!—
                                                    (ll. 2072–81)
["Hear me, my courtiers, counts and lords!
I wish to make a request of my Cid the Battler;
may Christ ensure that it brings him advantage!
I ask you to give your daughters, Doña Elvira and
                                                    Doña Sol,
as wives to the Infantes of Carrión.
I consider the marriage to be honourable and to bring
                                                    great prestige;
the Infantes ask it of you and I command it.
In both parties, let all those present,
both my men and yours, join me in the request.
Give them to us, My Cid, so may the Creator protect
                                                    you!"]

Move 2 (Cantar III)

Move 2 involves the resolution of a question of honor afflicting King Alfonso as a consequence of the flogging and the abandonment of the daughters of the Cid at Corpes by the infantes of Carrión.

The symbolic transcription of Move 2 appears below:

$$\S\{a\}BC\{\uparrow G^2\}o{:}M{:}N{:}\{K^4\}$$

(The above symbolic transcription corresponds to the numerical functions: {VIIIa}, IX, X, {XI, XV}, XXIII, XXV, XXVI, and {XIX})

The infantes' flogging and abandonment of their wives at Corpes creates a question of honor for both the Cid and King Alfonso. As the Cid avers to Muño Gustioz, whom he will shortly send as his emissary to the king to bring grievances against his former two sons-in-law, the assault perpetrated by don Fernando and don Diego at Corpes against his daughters has dishonored him, but more so King Alfonso, since it was the king who had insisted on marrying the Cid's daughters to the brothers of Carrión.

When next Muño Gustioz visits with the king at Sahagún—the latter constitutes a connective link (§)—he purposely decides to limit his conversation with don Alfonso to the topic of honor so as to intensify the king's guilt in this affair. Indeed, Muño Gustioz places the Cid's dishonor squarely on the king's shoulders. Stylistically sofisticated, Muño Gustioz's discourse reveals the use of the figures polyptoton ("Casastes" / "casamiento," "majaron" / "majadas"), alliteration (of the consonants "k," "s," "m," and "d"), prozeugma (of the verbs: "dexaron" and "levedes"), isocolon ("a las bestias" / "a las aves"), alloiosis (indicating alternatives by the conjunction "or": "o a juntas o a cortes"), and tricolon ("a vistas" / "a juntas" / "a cortes"). Note the cruel irony of the words of Muño Gustioz with respect to the honor—that is, dishonor—that the forced marriages of don Rodrigo's daughters to the infantes of Carrión have inflicted upon don Rodrigo and his family in line 2941: "Ya vós sabedes la ondra   que es cuntida a nós:"

—Casastes sus fijas   con ifantes de Carrión,
alto fue el casamiento,   ca lo quisieste vós.
Ya vós sabedes la ondra   que es cuntida a nós,
cuémo nos han abiltados   ifantes de Carrión.
Mal majaron sus fijas   del Cid Campeador,
majadas e desnudas   a grande desonor,
desenparadas las dexaron   en el robredo de Corpes
a las bestias fieras   e a las aves del mont.
Afelas sus fijas   en Valencia, do son.
Por esto vos besa las manos   commo vassallo a
 señor
que ge los levedes a vistas   o a juntas o a cortes.
Tiénes' por desondrado,   mas la vuestra es mayor,
e que vos pese, rey,   commo sodes sabidor;
que aya mio Cid derecho   de ifantes de Carrión.—
(ll. 2939–52)

["You married his daughters to the Infantes of Carrión.
It was a prestigious marriage, for such was your wish.
You already know what great honour it has brought upon us;
how we have been insulted by the Infantes of Carrión.
Cruelly they beat the daughters of the Cid the Battler;
beaten and naked, in great dishonour,
they left them helpless in the oak-wood at Corpes,
at the mercy of the wild beasts and the birds of the forest.
See how his daughters are now in Valencia.
For this reason he kisses your hands, as vassal to lord,
and requests that you take the Infantes to meet him at an assembly or at a royal court.
He considers himself dishonoured, but your dishonour is greater.
May this fill you with sadness, since you are wise in the law!
Let My Cid have justice of the Infantes of Carrión!"]

In turn, King Alfonso, after listening to the Cid's emissary, does not shirk from assuming responsibility for what has transpired at Corpes and, thereby, tacitly admits his need to recover his honor in this affair {a}—stylistically, note the sense of gravity of this scenic moment that the narrator conveys to his or her reader by his use of a double parelcon ("grand hora" and "calló / comidio"); note, furthermore, don Alfonso's use of the figures polyptoton ("casé" / "casamiento," "digo" / "dizes"), alliteration (of the consonant sounds "k'" and "s"), and repetitio ("verdad" / "verdad")—:

El rey una grand ora   calló e comidió:
—Verdad te digo yo   que me pesa de coraçón
e verdad dizes en esto   tú, Muño Gustioz,
ca yo casé sus fijas   con ifantes de Carrión,
fizlo por bien   que fuesse a su pro;
¡siquier el casamiento   fecho non fuesse oy!

Entre yo e mio Cid pésanos de coraçón,
ayudarl'é a derecho, sí n' salve el Criador.—
(ll. 2953–60)
[For a good hour the King reflected in silence:
"I tell you in truth that I am deeply saddened;
you speak the truth in this, Muño Gustioz,
for I married his daughters to the Infantes of Carrión.
I did it seeking good, that it might be to his advantage.
Today, I wish that I had not brought about the marriage!
Both I and My Cid are deeply saddened;
I shall help him obtain justice, may the Creator save me!"]

    To resolve grievances that the Cid wishes to raise against don Fernando and don Diego, King Alfonso holds court in Toledo (BC)—tacit is the king's depature for Toledo and the spatial transference between two kingdoms by land {↑G^2}. At this point, two messengers, one from the infante of Navarre and another from the infante of Aragón, suddenly appear unrecognized on the scene (o:)—this constitutes a flagrant deus ex machina incident since nothing in the text structurally justifies their presence at this juncture of the epic poem—who request that the Cid allow his two daughters to marry the infante of Navarre and the infante of Aragón. The latter creates a difficult task for the Cid (M), since its direct fulfillment would oblige him to defy King Alfonso, the ultimate authority in whom such matters are vested.

Assí commo acaban esta razón,
afé dos cavalleros entraron por la cort,
al uno dizen Oiarra e al otro Yéñego Simenoz,
el uno es del ifante de Navarra e el otro del ifante de Aragón,
besan las manos al rey don Alfonso,
piden sus fijas a mio Cid el Campeador
por ser reinas de Navarra e de Aragón,

e que ge las diessen a ondra e a bendición.
(ll. 3392, 3395–96, 3400)
[Just as these words have been said,
behold two knights coming into the court;
one is called Ojarra, and the other Íñigo Jiménez;
the one is an emissary from the Prince of Navarre,
and the other from the Prince of Aragón.
They kiss King Don Alfonso's hands,
and ask for the daughters of My Cid the Battler,
to be queens of Navarre and Aragón.
They ask that they be given to them in honour and
with holy blessing.]

Don Rodrigo resolves the issue by involving the king directly in the decision making process, thus transferring the difficult task to don Alfonso (M): "—sin vuestro mandado nada non feré yo—" (l. 3408) ["'Without your command, I shall do nothing'"]. King Alfonso, of course, immediately grants his consent (N), thereby resolving the pressing issue facing his vassal:

—Ruégovos, Cid, caboso Campeador,
que plega a vós, e atorgarlo he yo.
Este casamiento oy se otorgue en esta cort,
ca crécevos ý ondra e tierra e onor.—
(ll. 3410–13)
["I ask you, O Cid, worthy Battler,
to consent to this; I shall grant it.
Let permission for this marriage be given today in
this court,
for by it you gain in honour, possessions and lands."]

Note that by virtue of his granting don Rodrigo his request, don Alfonso at the same time liquidates the cumbersome stigma regarding his dishonor brought about by the savage comportment of infantes of Carrión against the daughters of the Cid in the forest of Corpes—the resolution of the difficult task (N) here assimilates the function of the liquidation of the initial misfortune ($\{K^4\}$).

Tale 18: The Tale of the Infante of Navarre
Tale 18 is a single-move tale that takes place at the close of Cantar III. Below is the symbolic transcription of Move 1:

$$aBCw^1\{\uparrow G^2\}W^*\{\downarrow\}$$

(The above symbolic transcription corresponds to the numerical functions: VIIIa, IX, X, XXXI, {XI, XV}, XXXI, and {XX}.)
This is a deus ex machina tale. The infante of Navarre lacks a wife (a^1) and sends an emissary to King Alfonso's court in Toledo to seek the consent of the Cid to marry one of his daughters (B). With approval of King Alfonso, the Cid consents (C) to the marriage proposed by the messenger of the infante of Navarre—the latter constitutes a promised marriage (w^1). Subsequently, the infante of Navarre marries one of the daughters of the Cid in Valencia (W*)—tacit, hence, is his departure from his estate, his spatial transference between territories by land, and his return to his kingdom with his wife ($\{\uparrow G^2\downarrow\}$).

Tale 19: The Tale of the Infante of Aragón
Tale 19 is a single-move tale that takes place at the close of Cantar III. Below is the symbolic transcription of Move 1:

$$aBCw^1\{\uparrow G^2\}W^*\{\downarrow\}$$

(The above symbolic transcription corresponds to the numerical functions: VIIIa, IX, X, XXXI, {XI, XV}, XXXI, and {XX}.)
This is a deus ex machina tale. The infante of Aragón lacks a wife (a^1) and sends an emissary to King Alfonso's court in Toledo to seek the consent of the Cid to marry one of his daughters (B). With approval of King Alfonso, the Cid consents (C) to the marriage proposed by the messenger of the infante of Aragón—the latter constitutes a promised marriage (w^1). Subsequently, the infante of Aragón marries one of the daughters of the Cid in Valencia (W*)—tacit, hence, is his departure from his estate, his spatial transference between territories by land, and his return to his kingdom with his wife ($\{\uparrow G^2\downarrow\}$).

Notes

Chapter 1. Preliminary Remarks

[1] The first English translation of Propp's study on the Russian fairy tale: *Morfológija skázki* (Leningrad: Academia, 1928), was published in the late 1950s: *Morphology of the Folktale*, trans. Lawrence Scott, introd. Svatava Pirkova-Jakobson (Bloomington: Research Center, Indiana University, 1958). In 1968 Luis A. Wagner published the second revised English edition (Austin: University of Texas Press), in which he retained Pirkova-Jakobson's introductory comments to the first edition (xix–xxii) and presented a new introduction by Alan Dundes (xi–xvii). My references to the *Morphology* are to Wagner's 1968 edition, and will be incorporated parenthetically in the text.

[2] *Cantar de Mio Cid*, ed., Alberto Montaner Frutos; all subsequent references to the *Cantar de Mio Cid* will be to this edition and will be included parenthetically in the text. Analysis of the syntagmatic, narrative structure in the *Cantar de Mio Cid* is absent in: Edmund de Chasca, *Arte juglaresco en el "Cantar de Mio Cid"*; Ramón Menéndez Pidal, *Cantar de Mio Cid: Texto, gramática y vocabulario*; Ramón Menéndez Pidal, introduction, *Poema de Mio Cid* 7–97; and Colin Smith, *The Making of the "Poema de Mio Cid."* It receives short shrift in Juan Carlos Conde, introduction, *Cantar de Mio Cid* 33–76; Francisco A. Marcos Marín, introduction, *Cantar de Mio Cid* 9–111; Ian Michael, introduction, *Poema de Mio Cid* 11–64; Colin Smith, introduction, *Poema de Mio Cid* (1972) xiii–xcviii; and Colin Smith, introduction, *Poema de Mio Cid* (1993) 17–118. To the best of my knowledge, four studies focus specifically on the organizational aspect of events in the *Cantar de Mío Cid*. The first is Eugene Dorfman's *The Narreme in the Medieval Romance Epic. An Introduction to Narrative Structures*; the second is Aristóbulo Pardo's "La trayectoria de Mio Cid y la armadura del poema;" the third is Ernesto Porras Collantes's "Descripción funcional del *Cantar de Mio Cid*;" and the fourth is Alberto Montaner Frutos's "El Cid: Mito y símbolo."

Dorfman posits four core contextual grounds of the *Cantar de Mio*

Cid, the sum of which constitute the substructure of the epic poem. Then he undertakes a macro-structural analysis of the same—that is, of the four fundamental component incidents or narremes (6–7) of the *Cantar de Mio Cid*. These four narremic events, regulated by the structural principle of cause-effect, gyrate around the domestic life of don Rodrigo. According to Dorfman, these four kernel occurrences are: (1) the cowardly behavior of the infantes of Carrión in the escaped lion episode, which Dorfman mistakenly labels as a family quarrel between the Cid and his sons-in-law; (2) the subsequent derision that don Fernando and don Diego endure from the members of don Rodrigo's court; (3) the barbarous affront that the infantes of Carrión commit against doña Elvira and doña Sol in the woods of Corpes; and (4) King Alfonso's decision to try don Fernando and don Diego for their aforementioned actions. Events preceding these four key events—that is, the exile of the Cid, don Rodrigo's subsequent victories over Moorish forces that bring him military fame, his subsequent conquest of Valencia, his subsequent reconciliation with King Alfonso, his acquisition of wealth, and the marriages of the Cid's daughters to the infantes of Carrión—constitute the "Expansion: The Prologue" (197). Those that follow the key narremic episodes—that is, the incidents in which the royal court passes judgments on the infantes, the three duels or "trials by combat," and the "final punishment" of don Fernando and don Diego that force the two brothers of Carrión to "relinquish their gains," that brand them as "infamous cowards and traitors," and oblige them to "serve their former wives who are now their superiors in rank" (198)—constitute the "Expansion: The Epilogue" (198). In short, Dorfman does not render a functional, micro-structural Proppian analysis of the episodes that make up the Prologue, "[t]he Autonomous Core System: The Main Plot" (198), and the Epilogue. Furthermore, he fails to elaborate and justify why certain aspects of actions constitute minor, marginal segmental interludes, incidents that pertain to the superstructure of the epic poem, whose omission, "however poetic, delightful, entertaining, artistic, and otherwise memorable they may be" (7), would not negatively impact the organically related chronological progression of "the central core of the action" (133) in the *Cantar de Mio Cid*.

Neither the study of Aristóbulo Pardo ("La trayectoria de Mio Cid y la armadura del poema") nor that of Ernesto Porras Collantes ("Descripción funcional del *Cantar de Mio Cid*") renders the number of the tales that constitute the exile of the Cid section of the poem nor do they concern themselves with the functions of the dramatis personae. Pardo stresses, for example, the motivational and affective psychological states of characters from the perspective of the victors; the Cid's knowledge of the geographical terrain of Arab lands; the outcome of the efforts of the Cid to regain the favor of don Alfonso—not the organization of the functions that constitute its structure—; and religion and its importance in the epic poem. Porras Collantes, in turn, presents extensive graphics, displaying relations that underscore elements of discord–harmony, opposition–similarity, broken–mended relationships between sets of characters and groups—between the Cid–King Alfonso, the friends of the Cid–friends of King Alfonso, the Cid–García Ordóñez, etc.

Lastly, there is Montaner Frutos's "El Cid: mito y símbolo." His Proppian analysis of the *Cantar de Mio Cid* (312–27), paradoxically, differs significantly from mine. Montaner Frutos renders the epic poem strictly as a single tale, that of don Rodrigo, the Cid, whereas I contend that the *Cantar de Mio Cid* constitutes a composite of nineteen tales (see chapter 2). He fails, also, to divide his morphological analysis of the tale of the Cid into moves. His Proppian interpretations of the functions in the Cid tale lead him to posit schematic formulas that do not coincide with my morphological analysis of the syntagmatic structure of the Spanish epic poem. The following comparison of identical incidents demonstrate how our functional interpretations differ. Take Montaner Frutos's rendition of the missing initial episode of the exile of the Cid that Menéndez Pidal provides in prose for the reader up to the moment when don Rodrigo, exiled by King Alfonso, departs from Vivar en route to Burgos (*Poema de Mio Cid* 99–102). Montaner Frutos unjustifiably simplifies Menendez Pidal's prose version of this initial event, an interpretive flaw on his part, that leads him to posit the following erroneous symbolic rendition of this episode (315):

$$\alpha x \xi L \eta A^9 \theta^1 \gamma^2 a^6$$

Montaner Frutos' disorderly symbolic organization of functions that unexpectedly jut forward and, then, unexpectedly move backward, contradicts Propp's contention that the functions of incidents within a unit of action follow a progressive, linear order (see my chapters 1 and 2). Below is my functional interpretation of Menéndez Pidal's opening prose summary:

$$\{\alpha\beta\gamma\delta A^{19}C\uparrow G^2 H^1\downarrow :o\text{-LMN-ExU}\}$$

(For an explanation of my above symbolic, functional interprretation, see Chapter 3. The Tale of the Exile of Rodrigo Díaz, the Cid. Move 1.)

Or take Montaner Frutos's interpretive rendition of a passage on which we appear to agree; however, first impressions can be deceiving. The incident in question refers to don Rodrigo's successful defense of Alcocer against a counterattack by Moorish forces led by King Fáriz and King Galve. Note that the second part of the formula, which commences with A^{19}, constitutes a subset of a difficult task (M) and its resolution (N). Following is Montaner Frutos's symbolic transcription of this event (316):

$$M, N = A^{19}H^1J^1[sic]K^4w^3$$

(Throughout his morphological analysis, Montaner Frutos equivocally renders the letter "J" to symbolize function XVIII, the defeat of the villain or victory. For Propp the letter "I" represents the latter, whereas the letter "J", in turn, denotes function XVII: the marking or wounding of the hero—*Morphology* 52–53. Also, throughout his study, Montaner Frutos renders Propp's symbolic transcription "$w°$:" function XXXI: the hero receives a monetary reward or an equivalent compensation as his final award [Propp 64], as "w^3.") In the above subset battle in an open field (H^1) Montaner Frutos subsequently mentions as an aside Minaya Álvar Fáñez's losing his horse: a^2, and don Rodrigo immediately providing him with another: $D^9E^9F^1K^4$. Now, if the latter encounter pertains to the functions M and N, then it follows that all battle scenes following the initial one of Castejón in the exile of the Cid tale constitute, as well, subsets of M and N. Here Montaner Frutos errs because he ignores a key point that Propp makes in his *Morphology*—namely, that "within a single tale any new occurrence of villainy (A) or lack (a) gives rise to a new move" (92).

Since the Cid's decision to defend Alcocer constitutes don Rodrigo's response to an act of villainy, which the above Moorish kings commit by declaring war on the Cid (A^{19}), this event marks the beginning of a new move—my Move 7 of the Tale of the Exile of Rodrigo Díaz, the Cid. Hence, it is a grave mistake to postulate, as Montaner Frutos does, that this occurrence falls under the rubric of a difficult task (M) and its resolution (N). The latter misinterpretation on Montaner Frutos's part immediately, and unnecessarily, obliges him to complicate the issue by forcing him to supply subsequently a subset of functions to clarify the function XXV (M) and function XXVI (N), respectively. Simply put, the Minaya Álvar Fáñez poetic interlude forms an integral part of the battle scene in an open field (H^1). Hence, I render the symbolic transcription of the above event as follows:

$$A^{19}BC{\uparrow}H{:}^1I{:}^1K^4{\downarrow}w^o{:}$$

(It is evident that Montaner Frutos's interpretation of Propp, as applied to the *Cantar de Mio Cid*, differs markedly from my Proppian analysis of the epic poem. Henceforth, I shall limit my comparisons with Montaner Frutos's symbolic rendition of the functions of the *Cantar de Mio Cid* to Chapter 3. The Tale of the Exile of Rodrigo Díaz, the Cid (Moves 2–5) and incorporate his symbolic transcriptions in the Notes.)

To bring this extensive notational review of the morphologic disparity between Montaner Frutos's and my Proppian interpretation of the *Cantar de Mio Cid* to a close, it would appear that there are as many interpretations of a text "as there are readers" (Fish 305).

[3] Propp's work has influenced many theorists, scholars, and critics in literary criticism and the social sciences such as: Manuel Alvar, Anita Benaim de Lasry, A. J. Greimas, Claude Bremond, Alan Dundes, Carlos Foresti, William O. Hendricks, David Herman, Jack J. Himelblau, Elli Köngä Maranda and Pierre Maranda, Alberto Montaner Frutos, and Victor D. Montejo.

[4] English translations of passages from the *Cantar de Mio Cid* in brackets ([ ]) are to Peter Such's and John Hodgkinson's *Poem of My Cid*; English translations of the *Cantar de Mio Cid* in braces ({ }) are mine.

[5] The following two apostrophes: "Oíd qué dixo Minaya Álbar Fáñez" (l. 1127) {"Listen to what Minaya Álvar Fáñez said"} and "Aqueste era el rey Búcar si l'oviestes contar" (l. 2314) ["This was the Emir Búcar; perhaps you have heard tell of him"], contain assonant-paroxytone interior rhymes of "a-a" and "e-e," respectively: "Minaya" / "Álvar" and "Aqueste" / "oviestes." In the *Cantar de Mio Cid*, interior rhyme in the same line or in consecutive lines is not uncommon. In the present study my references to rhyme, unless otherwise noted, are always to interior rhyme. A rhyme is assonant when, after the last accented vowel, only the vowels in the corresponding rhyming words are identical (for

example: "Minaya" / "Álvar, " "Aqueste" / "oviestes," "pagados" / "fincamos"); a rhyme is consonant when all the letters following the last accented vowel are the same (for example: "dado" / "pagado;" "ovo" / "tovo," "foradar" / "pasar"). A rhyme is feminine when the words that rhyme are paroxytones (for example: "Minaya" / "Álvar," "Aqueste" / "oviestes," "pagados" / "fincamos"); the rhyme is masculine when the words that rhyme are oxytones (for example: "foradar" / "pasar," "Criador" / "Campeador"). The majority of the interior rhyme patterns in the *Cantar de Mio Cid* are assonant and paroxytone. For an in-depth enumeration of rhyme patterns in the *Cantar de Mio Cid*, see Menéndez Pidal, *Crítica del texto* (1944), 1: 103–24 and De Chasca 219–36.

Chapter 3. The Tale of the Exile of Rodrigo Díaz, the Cid

[1] Editions with the same or similar summary to that of Menéndez Pidal are those of, for example, Conde, *Cantar de Mio Cid* 88–96; Marcos Marín *Cantar de Mio Cid* 163–67; Smith *Poema de Mio Cid* (1972) 1–2; and Smith *Poema de Mio Cid* (1993) 135–36.

[2] Harriet Goldberg (*Motif-Index* 145, Q431.20) observes that the banishment of a slandered hero is a Spanish medieval, folkloric motif. My references to passages from the *Cantar de Mio Cid* that constitute medieval folkloric motifs are to Goldberg's *Motif-Index* compilation.

[3] Montaner Frutos's symbolic transcription of this episode follows (315):

$$\delta^2 B^2 \uparrow F^6 \gamma^1 a^5 \text{contr.} \ \delta^1 = \delta^2 \text{neg.} Ka^5 \delta^1 Ka^6 a^5 D^{10} E^{10} Kf^1 Mw^3 a^6 D \uparrow$$

[4] The omen of birds, good (on the right) and / or bad (on the left), is another Spanish medieval folkloric motif; Goldberg 5, B147.2.2.1.1.

[5] Stylistic terms are from Richard A. Lanham's *A Handlist of Rhetorical Terms*. In this study I do not italicize the nomenclature of rhetorical terms.

[6] Cheating by substitution of valuables with worthless articles is another Spanish medieval folkloric motif; Goldberg 96, K476.2.

[7] Another Spanish medieval folkloric motif is that of moneylenders who others deceive; Goldberg 83, J1510.2; Goldberg 105, K1667.2; and Goldberg 131, P435.15.

[8] The symbolic transcription of this occurrence by Montaner Frutos is given below:

a contr. a⁵RsDEβ

⁹ For the analysis of Tale 2. The Tale of Doña Jimena, the Wife of Rodrigo Díaz, see the Appendix.

¹⁰ For the analysis of Tale 3. The Tale of Doña Elvira and Doña Sol, the Daughters of Doña Jimena and Rodrigo Díaz, see the Appendix.

¹¹ For the analysis of Doña Jimena's prayer to Christ, see the Appendix.

¹² The prophetic dream is a Spanish medieval folkloric motif; Goldberg 120, M312.10 and Goldberg 198, V510.9.

¹³ Montaner Frutos's symbolic transcription of this incident, which commences with the Cid's dream in which the angel Gabriel appears and terminates with don Rodrigo's conquest of Alcocer, follows (315–16):

$$FC,G^2C\upharpoonleft <M,NMNw^3PrRs^1M,N$$

¹⁴ The symbolic transcription of this event by Montaner Frutos appears below (316):

$$M,N=A^{19}H^1J^1[sic]K^4\ a^2D^9E^9F^1K^4w^3$$

¹⁵ For the analysis of Tale 4. The King of Valencia's Counterattack against the Cid, see the Appendix.

¹⁶ For the analysis of Tale 5. Gestures by the Cid to Regain the Good Will of King Alfonso (Move 1), see the Appendix.

¹⁷ For the analysis of Tale 6. The Failure of Ramón Berenguer, Count of Barcelona, to Regain Lands Lost to the Cid, see the Appendix.

¹⁸ For the analysis of Tale 7. The Reaction of the Residents of Valencia against the Cid, see the Appendix.

¹⁹ For the analysis of Tale 8. The Failure of the King of Seville to Retake Valencia, see the Appendix.

²⁰ For the analysis of Tale 5: Gestures by the Cid to Regain the Good Will of King Don Alfonso (Move 2), see the Appendix.

²¹ For the analysis of Tale 9. The Tale of Raquel and Vidas, see the Appendix.

²² For the analysis of Tale 2. The Tale of Doña Jimena, the Wife of Rodrigo Díaz, see the Appendix.

²³ For the analysis of Tale 3. The Tale of Doña Elvira and Doña

Sol, the Daughters of Doña Jimena and Rodrigo Díaz (Move 1), see the Appendix.

[24] For the analysis of Tale 10. The Failure of King Yúsuf of Morocco to Recapture Valencia, see the Appendix.

[25] For the analysis of Tale 5: Gestures by the Cid to Regain the Good Will of King Alfonso (Move 3), see the Appendix.

Chapter 4. The Tale of Don Fernando González and Don Diego González, the Infantes of Carrión

[1] The arrangement of a marriage by a ruler is still another Spanish medieval folkloric motif; Goldberg 158, T61.4.6.

[2] For the analysis of Tale 3: The Tale of Doña Elvira and Doña Sol, the Daughters of Doña Jimena and Rodrigo Díaz (Move 2), see the Appendix.

[3] The cowardly behavior of courtiers is a Spanish medieval folkloric motif; Goldberg 203, W121.9.

[4] For the analysis of Tale 12. The Tale of the Cid's Handling of the Loose Lion Incident, see the Appendix.

[5] For the analysis of Tale 13. The Tale of the Cid's Victory over the Moroccan King Búcar, see the Appendix.

[6] For the analysis of Tale 14. The Tale of the Attempt by the Moroccan King Búcar to Reconquer Valencia, see the Appendix.

[7] The knights' negative reaction to don Fernando's words is in part justified. The Cid, and not the infantes, killed King Búcar. The other view that the narrator expresses on behalf of the knights—namely, that they had not espied don Fernando and don Diego combating the Moors—does not hold. Although the text does not present any grounds for doubting the veracity of the Cid's and Minaya Álvar Fáñez's positive illocutionary assertions, the reader may choose to place their commentaries in aporia. What the reader cannot question are judgments proffered by an omniscient narrator, since they are incontrovertible. As I have already indicated, the omniscient narrator has spoken and sided in favor of don Fernando and don Diego: "lidiaron de coraçon" (l. 2508). Consequently, the reaction of the Cid's vassals in lines 2532–34 is structurally unwarranted. From a critical point of view, the above incident reveals a rare paradox in the *Cantar de Mio Cid*—that is, a situation in which the omniscient narrator is unreliable.

[8] For the analysis of Tale 15. The Tale of the Moor Abengalbón's Encounter with the Infantes of Carrión, see the Appendix.
[9] A husband's cruelty toward his wife is a Spanish medieval folkloric motif; Goldberg 154, S62.5.
[10] For the analysis of Tale 3: The Tale of Doña Elvira and Doña Sol, the Daughters of Doña Jimena and Rodrigo Díaz (Move 3), see the Appendix.

Chapter 5. The Tale of the Revenge of the Cid on the Infantes of Carrión and the Remarriage of Doña Elvira and Doña Sol to the Infante of Navarre and Infante of Aragón

[1] Before replying to the Cid's queries, Count García attempts to deflect the issue with a brief observation regarding the Cid's long beard: "—Vezós' mio Cid   a llas cortes pregonadas. / Dexóla crecer   e luenga trae la barba, / los unos le han miedo   e los otros espanta—" (ll. 3272–74) ["'My Cid has grown too accustomed to such solemn courts. / He has allowed his beard to grow, and wears it long. / Some are afraid of him, others he fills with terror'"]. Don Rodrigo, subsequently, is quick to reply, recounting how in the past he had pulled out clumps of Count García's beard at the castle of Cabra:

—¿Qué avedes vós, conde,   por retraer la mi
                                                    barba?
Ca de cuando nasco   a delicio fue criada,
ca non me priso a ella   fijo de mugier nada
nimbla messó fijo   de moro nin de cristiana,
commo yo a vós, conde,   en el castiello de Cabra,
cuando pris a Cabra   e a vós por la barba.
Non ý ovo rapaz   que non messó su pulgada,
la que yo messé   aún non es eguada.—
                                        (ll. 3283–90)
["What reason have you, Count, to criticise my
                                                    beard?
For since it started to grow it has been tended with
                                                great care.
No son of woman has ever caught me by it,
nor has any son of Moor or Christian ever plucked it,

> as I did to you, Count, in the castle of Cabra.
> When I took Cabra, and pulled you by the beard,
> there was no young child who did not pluck his bit.
> The piece which I plucked has not yet properly
> grown."]

The Cid's response constitutes a fine example of an antistrephon [an argument that turns the words employed by one's opponent against the opponent himself] and a chleuasmos [a reply sarcastic in nature that mocks one's adversary]. The pulling of a person's beard constitutes an insult to one's victim and is a Spanish medieval folkloric motif; Goldberg 133, P672.

[2] For the analysis of Tale 17. The Tale of King Alfonso, see the Appendix.

[3] I render Propp's symbol of a fiancée who ascends the throne upon getting married as W:.

[4] For the analysis of Tale 3: The Tale of Doña Elvira and Doña Sol, the Daughters of Doña Jimena and Rodrigo Díaz (Move 4), see the Appendix.

[5] For the analysis of Tale 18. The Tale of the Infante of Navarre, see the Appendix.

[6] For the analysis of Tale 19. The Tale of the Infante of Aragón, see the Appendix.

Chapter 6. Conclusion

[1] This, in turn, raises the following question, a question, indeed, of no small interest: Are all folk epics extended fairy tales?

[2] Roman Jakobson uses such phrases as "eminent study" (*Dialogues* 16) and "pioneering monograph" ("Closing Statement" 374) to refer to Propp's *Morphology*. The latter seminal treatise has universal implications that Jakobson is quick to note. According to Jakobson, Propp has shown not only that there is a "limited choice of plots" (*Dialogues* 16), but also "how a consistently syntactic approach may be of paramount help even in classifying the traditional plots and in tracing the puzzling laws that underlie their composition and selection" ("Closing Statement" 374). Besides the examples already given from the exile of the Cid and from the

Popol Vuh and from Asturias's *El Señor Presidente* (1946), I here offer two additional cases to substantiate even further Jakobson's abovementioned view. The first has to do with Victor D. Montejo's recorded tales from his native rural Guatemalan Jacaltenango, Huehuetenago ("Enseñanza de la fábula"); the second refers to rural folk tales of magic collected in Chile by Carlos Foresti (*Análisis morfológico*). In both instances, the morphologic structure of the tales coincides with those delineated by Propp for the Russian fairy tales.

Works Consulted

Aarne, Antti, and Stith Thompson. *The Types of the Folk-Tale. A Classification and Bibliography* (1928). Enlarged ed. Trans. Stith Thompson. New York: Franklin, 1971.

Alvar, Manuel. *Estudios. "Libro de Apolonio:" Estudios, ediciones y concordancias*. Vol. 1. Valencia: Fundación March; Castalia, 1976. 212–36.

Aristotle. *On the Art of Poetry with a Supplement on Music*. 1948. Trans. S. H. Butcher. Ed. and introd. Milton C. Nahm. The Library of Liberal Arts 6. New York: Liberal Arts Press, 1956.

Austin, J. L. *How to Do Things with Words: The William James Lectures Delivered at Harvard University in 1955*. Ed. J. O. Urmson. New York: Oxford University Press, 1973.

Bandera Gómez, Cesáreo. *El "Poema de Mío Cid": Poesía, historia, mito*. Biblioteca Románica Hispánica II. Estudios y Ensayos 124. Madrid: Gredos, 1969.

Benaim de Lasry, Anita. *Carlos Maynes and La enperatrís de Roma. Critical Edition and Study of Two Medieval Spanish Romances*. Newark, DE: Juan de la Cuesta, 1982. 73–82.

Booth, Wayne C. *The Rhetoric of Fiction*. Chicago: University of Chicago Press, 1961.

Bremond, Claude. *Logique de récit*. Paris: Seuil, 1973.

———. "La logique des possibles narratifs." *Communications* 8 (1966): 60–76.

———. "Le message narratif." *Communications* 4 (1964): 4–32.

Burgos, Fernando, ed. and Presentación. *Studies in Honor of Myron Lichtblau*. Homenajes 16. Newark, DE: Juan de la Cuesta, 2000.

Conde, Juan Carlos, ed. and introd. *Cantar de Mio Cid*. Texto antiguo Ramón Menéndez Pidal. Prosificación moderna Alfonso Reyes. Prólogo Martín de Riquer. 1976. 26th ed. Colección Austral 20. Madrid: Espasa-Calpe, 2004.

———. Introduction. By Conde 33–76.

De Chasca, Edmund. *El Arte juglaresco en el "Cantar de Mio Cid."* 1955. Augmented 2nd ed. Biblioteca Románica Hispánica II. Estudios y

Ensayos 101. Madrid: Gredos, 1972.
Dorfman, Eugene. *The Narreme in the Medieval Romance Epic. An Introduction to Narrative Structures*. University of Toronto Romance Series 13. Toronto: University of Toronto Press, 1969.
Dundes, Alan. "From Etic to Emic Units in the Structural Study of Folktales." *Journal of American Folklore* 75 (1962): 95–105.
———. *The Morphology of North American Indian Folktales*. Folklore Fellows Communications 195. Helsinki: Suomalainen Tiedeakatemia, 1964.
———. New introd. Propp xi–xvii.
———. "Structural Typology in North American Indian Folktales." *The Study of Folklore*. Ed. Alan Dundes. Englewood Cliffs, NJ: Prentice, 1965. 206–15.
Fish, Stanley. *Is there a Text in This Class? The Authority of Interpretive Communities*. Cambridge, MA: Harvard University Press, 1980.
Foresti, Carlos. *Análisis morfológico de veinte cuentos de magia de la tradición oral chilena. Aplicación y discusión del método de Vladimir Propp*. Goteborg: Romanica Gothoburgensia, 1985.
Goldberg, Harriet. *Motif-Index of Medieval Spanish Folk Narratives*. Medieval and Renaissance Texts and Studies 162. Tempe: Arizona State University, 1998.
Greimas, A. J. *Sémantique structural: Langue et Langage*. Paris: Larousse, 1966.
Hendricks, William O. *Essays on Semiolinguistics and Verbal Art*. The Hague: Mouton, 1973.
———. "The Work and Play Structures of Narrative." *Semiotica* 13 (1975): 281–328.
Herman, David. "Scripts, Sequences, and Stories: Elements of a Postclassical Narratology." *PMLA* 112 (1997): 1046–59.
Himelblau, Jack J. "The *Cantar de Mio Cid*: A Morphological-Syntagmatic Analysis of the Exile of the Cid." *eHumanista: Journal of Medieval and Early Modern Iberian Studies* 6 (2006): 1–18 <http//www.ehumanista.ucsb.edu/>.
———. "The Cara de Ángel and Camila Narrative in M. A. Asturias's *El Señor Presidente*: Morphologic, Folkloric, and Psychoanalytical Observations." Burgos 141–62.
———. "M. A. Asturias's *El Señor Presidente*: A Morphological Analysis

of the Single-Move Micro Tales." Mendizábal and Fernández Jiménez 107–18.

———. "M. A. Asturias's *El Señor Presidente*: Chaos Begotten from Order." *Hispanófila* 135 (2002): 107–23.

———. "The Morphology of the Popol Vuh." 1989. Himelblau 49–64. Rpt. of "The Popol Vuh of the Maya Quiche: A Morphological Study." *Inter-American Review of Bibliography* 37 (1987): 480–500.

———. *Quiche Worlds in Creation: The Popol Vuh as a Narrative Work of Art*. Culver City, CA: Labyrinthos, 1989.

Ingarden, Roman. *The Cognition of the Literary Work of Art*. Northwestern University Studies in Phenomenology and Existential Philosophy. Trans. and introd. Ruth Ann Crowley and Kenneth R. Olson. Evanston, IL: Northwestern University Press, 1973.

Iser, Wolfgang. *The Act of Reading: A Theory of Aesthetic Response*. Baltimore: Johns Hopkins University Press, 1978.

———. *The Implied Reader: Patterns of Communication in Prose Fiction from Bunyan to Beckett*. Baltimore: Johns Hopkins University Press, 1974.

Jakobson, Roman. "Closing Statement: Linguistics and Poetics." Sebeok 350–77.

Jakobson, Roman, and Krystyna Pomorska. *Dialogues*. Trans. Christian Hubert. Cambridge, MA: MIT Press, 1983.

Jauss, Hans Robert. *Aesthetic Experience and Literary Hermeneutics*. Trans. Michael Shaw. Introd. Wlad Godzich. Theory and History of Literature 3. Minneapolis: University of Minnesota Press, 1982.

———. *Question and Answer: Forms of Dialogic Understanding*. Ed., trans., and forward by Michael Hays. Theory and History of Literature 68. Minneapolis: University of Minnesota Press, 1989.

———. *Toward an Aesthetic of Reception*. Trans. Timothy Bahti. Introd. Paul de Man. Theory and History of Literature 2. Minneapolis: University of Minnesota Press, 1982.

Köngäs Maranda, Elli, and Pierre Maranda. *Structural Models in Folklore and Transformational Essays*. Approaches to Semiotics 10. The Hague: Mouton, 1971.

Lanham, Richard A. *A Handlist of Rhetorical Terms.* 1968. 2nd ed. Berkeley: University of California Press, 1991.
Maranda, Pierre, and Elli Köngäs Maranda. "Structural Models in Folklore." Köngäs Maranda and Maranda 17–94.
Marcos Marín, Francisco A., ed. *Cantar de Mio Cid.* Clásicos de Biblioteca Nueva 2. Madrid: Biblioteca Nueva, 1997.
———. Introduction. By Marcos Marín 9–111.
Mendizábal, Juan Cruz and Juan Fernández Jiménez, eds. *Visión de la narrativa hispánica.* Indiana, PA: Indiana University of Pennsylvania, 1999.
Menéndez Pidal, Ramón. *Cantar de Mio Cid: Texto, gramática y vocabulario.* 1908-11. 4th ed. 3 vols. Madrid: Espasa-Calpe, 1964–1969.
———. *Crítica del texto.* 1964. Menéndez Pidal Vol. 1.
———, ed. *Texto del Cantar.* 1969. Menéndez y Pidal Vol. 3.
———, ed. *Poema de Mio Cid.* 1913. 11th ed. Clásicos Castellanos 24. Madrid: Espasa-Calpe, 1966.
———. Introduction. 1966. Menéndez Pidal 7–97.
Michael, Ian, ed. and introd. *Poema de Mio Cid.* 1984. 5th ed. Clásicos Castalia 75. Madrid: Castalia, 1991.
———. Introduction. By Michael 11–64.
Montaner Frutos, Alberto, ed. *Cantar de Mio Cid.* 1993. Prólogo y notas Alberto Montaner. Estudio preliminar Francisc o Rico. Biblioteca Clásica. Barcelona: Galaxia Gutenberg; Círculo de Lectores, 2007.
———. "El Cid: Mito y símbolo." *Boletín del Museo e Instituto "Camón Aznar"* 27 (1987): 121–340.
Montejo, Victor D. "La enseñanza de la fábula en la tradición indígena de Jacaltenango, Huehuetenango [Guatemala]." Paper presented at the Third International Symposium on Latin American Indian Literatures, Latin American Indian Literatures Association, San Antonio, Texas. March 30, 1985.
Pardo, Aristóbulo. "La trayectoria de Mio Cid y la armadura del poema." *Thesaurus* 28 (1973): 46–85.
Pirkova-Jakobson, Svatava. Introduction to the 1st ed. Propp xix–xxii.
Porras Collantes, Ernesto. "Descripción funcional del *Cantar de Mio Cid.*" *Thesaurus* 32 (1977): 660–91.

Propp, V. *Morphology of the Folktale.* 1958. 2nd rev. ed. Trans. Lawrence Scott. Ed. and pref. Louis A. Wagner. New introd. Alan Dundes. Introd. to 1st ed. Svatava Pirkova-Jackobson. American Folklore Society Bibliographical and Special Series 9. Austin: University of Texas Press, 1968.

Raglan, FitzRoy Richard Somerset. *The Hero: A Study in Tradition, Myth, and Drama.* 1936. New York: Vintage, 1956.

Searle, John R. *Speach Acts: An Essay in the Philosophy of Language.* 1969. New York: Cambridge University Press, 1977.

Sebeok, Thomas A., ed. *Style in Language.* Cambridge, MA: MIT Press, 1960.

Smith, Colin, ed. and introd. *Poema de Mio Cid.* Oxford: Claredon Press, 1972.

———, ed. and introd. *Poema de Mio Cid.* 1976. 18th ed. Letras Hispánicas 35. Madrid: Cátedra, 1993.

———. Introduction. 1972. By Smith xiii–xcviii.

———. Introduction. 1993. By Smith 17–118.

———. *The Making of the "Poema de Mio Cid."* Cambridge: Cambridge University Press, 1983.

Such, Peter and John Hodgkinson, trans., introd., and commentary. *Poem of My Cid.* Warminster: Aris and Phillips, 1987.

Weinrich, Harald. *Estructura y función de los tiempos en el lenguaje.* Trans. Federico Latorre. Biblioteca Románica Hispánica. II. Estudios y Ensayos 115. Madrid: Gredos, 1968.